Exploring
Iowa's Past

Exploring Iowa's Past
A Guide To
Prehistoric Archaeology

Lynn Marie Alex

University of Iowa Press
Iowa City, Iowa
1980

Library of Congress Cataloging in Publication Data

Alex, Lynn Marie, 1948–
    Exploring Iowa's past.

    Includes bibliographies.
    1. Indians of North America—Iowa—Antiquities.
2. Iowa—Antiquities. 3. Archaeology—
Methodology. I. Title.
E78.I6A43   977.7   80-21391
ISBN O-87745-108-7 (pbk.)

University of Iowa Press, Iowa City, Iowa 52242
© 1980 by The University of Iowa. All rights reserved
Printed in the United States of America

*To the Slatterys, Higgins, Pidcocks,
and other kindred Iowa spirits.*

Contents

Foreword

This guide is intended for those who wish to know more about Iowa archaeology and how they can become involved. We hope that everyone who reads it will better understand:

- ☐ What archaeology is and how it is related to anthropology.
- ☐ What archaeologists do and how this differs from the work of other scientists.
- ☐ The necessity of preserving Iowa's prehistoric heritage.
- ☐ How to recognize and report archaeological sites.
- ☐ What is wrong with the untrained person digging into an archaeological site.
- ☐ The purposes of archaeological survey and excavation.
- ☐ What skills are necessary to excavate archaeological sites.
- ☐ The importance of finding remains in context.
- ☐ Why all artifacts are important.
- ☐ The purposes of artifact classification.
- ☐ How to catalogue and store artifact collections.
- ☐ The development of archaeology in Iowa.
- ☐ The prehistoric culture sequence in Iowa.
- ☐ The Native American concern for sacred sites and how legislation is helping to protect these sites.
- ☐ Why archaeologists discourage the buying and selling of artifacts.
- ☐ What you can do to become involved in archaeology as a career or hobby.
- ☐ Where to go for more information.

Relief map of modern Iowa (Iowa Geological survey, 1975).

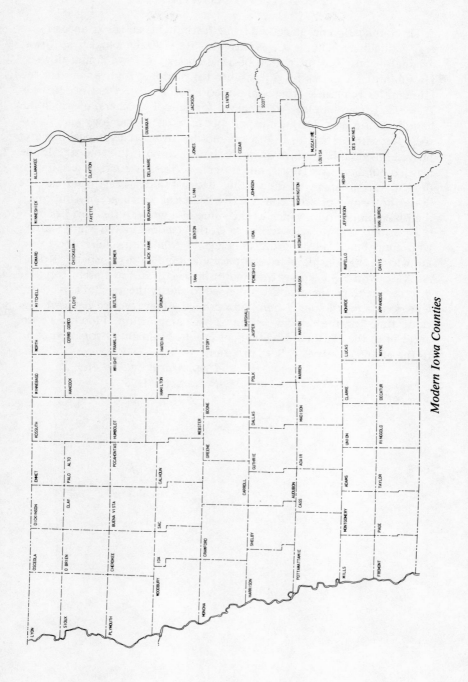

Modern Iowa Counties

Acknowledgments

This publication has benefited from the thoughts and assistance of several individuals. Duane C. Anderson, State Archaeologist of Iowa, originally conceived the notion of a handbook for Iowa archaeologists. He submitted a successful proposal to the National Endowment for the Humanities requesting financial support for a project entitled Iowa's P.A.S.T. (Programming Archaeology for School Teachers) of which the handbook is a part. His own experience in Iowa archaeology and his association with the Sanford Museum and the Iowa Archeological Society, proved invaluable in producing a manuscript of this nature. Blane Nansel, Julianne Loy Hoyer, and Joseph A. Tiffany contributed suggestions at various stages of the writing. Mona Walden-Frey proofread the initial draft and offered constructive criticism which greatly improved the final composition. Much of the value of a work of this sort lies in its illustrations, and we are grateful to Doris Macdonald and Mary Slattery who contributed most of the drawings. I would especially like to acknowledge the considerable assistance given me by my husband, Robert A. Alex, who has been my own major instructor in Iowa prehistory. He directed me to pertinent sources, helped to clarify the inevitable inconsistencies and gaps I found there, and proved a constructive critic when it came time for the scrutiny of my own composition. Finally, we are grateful to the National Endowment for the Humanities for its support to the entire Iowa's P.A.S.T. program.

Lynn Marie Betzler Alex
September, 1979

Introduction

Almost everyone is interested in archaeology. Whether it is the spirit of discovery, the lure of the exotic, or a fascination with the past, the idea of digging in the ground to recover information about ancient times intrigues most of us. While it is true that archaeology can be very exciting, it is misleading to think that most archaeological excavations are as well funded as the one that uncovered King Tutankhamen's tomb in Egypt, or as revolutionary as those conducted in Africa's Olduvai Gorge. Most archaeological research has been minimally financed, and excavation itself is hard work requiring continuous attention to detailed recording and mapping, and the careful recovery and analysis of sometimes meager and less than exotic finds. Nevertheless, each archaeological site provides added bits of information with which the past may be reconstructed.

In this handbook we will discuss what archaeology is and what archaeologists do. We hope that by reading it you will find answers to those questions archaeologists are often asked: "How do you know where to dig?" "How can you tell something is that old?" "How do you know that's a tool and not just another rock?" "When did people first come to Iowa?" We will describe the methods and techniques archaeologists use to recover prehistoric remains and how they describe, classify, and interpret them. While we intend to review the prehistoric cultures of our own state, you should keep in mind that modern political boundaries are a phenomena of recent historical events and have meaning in prehistory only as they correspond to natural features. Environmental boundaries such as rivers, mountain ranges, and vegetation zones are the significant features when interpreting the prehistoric sequence.

As an aid to self-instruction, each chapter in this handbook begins with a statement of its goals to help you concentrate on important areas of content. Key vocabulary and concepts are emphasized throughout and defined in the glossary at the end of the text. If you wish to pursue your interests in Iowa archaeology, the references listed at the end of each chapter provide suggestions for further reading.

Chapter 1

Archaeology

When we describe archaeology as the study of the past, people are often confused. Paleontologists and historians also study the past and they are not usually archaeologists. In this chapter we will explain what archaeology is and what archaeologists do. When you have completed it, you should understand the ways in which archaeology differs from these other disciplines.

Archaeology and the Concept of Culture

To begin, we must recognize that in the United States archaeology is considered a subfield of **anthropology**, the more encompassing "study of man." Although at many points, this broader discipline overlaps other fields of study, it is largely because of an emphasis on the importance of culture that anthropology remains distinct. Anthropologists believe that the human species has survived because of the degree to which we have developed, expanded, and become dependent on culture. **Culture** in this general sense, represents all of the patterns for living which humans have created in adapting to their environment, and which are transmitted from one generation to another. In the specific sense, culture is a society's "way of life." It includes material objects such as tools, clothing, houses, food, and transportation; as well as the non-material: behavior patterns, social organization, language, and beliefs. Yet, it is not just the presence of these material and nonmaterial aspects but the particular form they take in any one society that distinguishes one culture from another.

Culture is our means of adapting to our environment. Because of it, we wear clothing to keep warm while other animals grow heavy winter coats or travel southward to warmer climates. We retreat into our houses to the comfort of a warm fire and a good book rather than to a cave for winter hibernation. Because we live in Iowa and have adopted, or enculturated, the American way of life, in contrast to the citizen of Tokyo for instance, our house is more likely to be made of brick than of paper and wood, our fire is probably contained in a fire-place rather than a brazier, and our book is more likely written in English print, rather than in Japanese characters.

Culture is not inherited or instinctive. A child born of American parents but raised by a Japanese couple living in Tokyo will grow up speaking Japanese and practicing Japanese customs and behavior. You learn your culture by participating in it, through the example set by those around you, and as the result of direct communication, chiefly language. As a member of the human species, you **have** inherited the biological capacity for culture. You have a complex brain and central nervous system which permits symbolic, abstract thought and communication, as well as innovative behavior and an amazing capacity to learn. Your finely-tuned motor skills and anatomical structure gives you the potential of performing the tasks of a baseball pitcher or a brain surgeon. This biological basis for culture is the result of long-term developmental processes. Anthropologists believe that the key to understanding human behavior is in understanding the development of culture and how it has allowed us to cope with our environment in more and more complex ways.

Archaeology

Archaeologists are anthropologists who study the culture of extinct societies. The archaeologist adds time depth to the study of human behavior. Unlike ethnologists such as the late Margaret Mead, who spend time within a particular society and study its culture firsthand, archaeologists must find and recover the material remains left by former societies. From these they hope to reconstruct both the material and non-material aspects of culture.

People often say "archaeologists study old bones." In this they are partially correct. Archaeologists study the animal bones left by former societies to see what people ate. They also study the skeletal remains of the people themselves as these help us to understand what people looked like, and what diseases and injuries they suffered. But archaeologists spend more time analyzing the material remains left by ancient societies: the pottery, stone and bone tools, structures, field systems, and irrigation works. They believe that every culture is characterized by **regular patterns** of behavior, social organization, material items, and ideas which are shared by the members of the society. Although archaeologists cannot "dig up" the behavior patterns or ideas of prehistoric societies, they hope that the regularities in material remains they **can** recover, will help them to make inferences about the less visible aspects of extinct cultures.

Prehistoric archaeology

Like most disciplines, archaeology is specialized. **Prehistoric archaeologists** study preliterate cultures, those which left no written records. Without documentary evidence prehistoric archaeologists must rely solely on the material remains left by former societies. In North America, prehistory includes the entire interval of time prior to the arrival of Europeans, since no Native American society north of Mexico developed a system of writing.

With the arrival of Europeans in the late 15th century A.D., North America may be said to have entered the **proto-historic** period. After this point there are historical documents which occasionally provide written evidence of Native American societies with whom Europeans came in contact, but for many years these remained scanty and brief. Since the European expansion was gradual, some North American societies were not contacted for many years. Others were not documented at all. Therefore, for the proto-historic period, the archaeologist depends primarily on the material evidence of former societies, although occasionally there is textual information to supplement this data.

Historic archaeology

Some archaeologists are interested in societies for which there is well developed written documentation. We call them **historic archaeologists.** They share in the techniques and methodology common to our discipline in general, but have written records to supplement the archaeological data. In this respect, their work overlaps with that of the historian's. The goals of their research, however, remain fundamentally different from most historians, because, like other anthropologists, they are most interested in the reconstruction of the cultural and social aspects of former societies, rather than in describing and explaining the events and personalities of the times. For example, while we know who the Pilgrims were, and when and why they came to America as a result of historical research, archaeologists have been able to determine the original layout of Plymouth Colony, and the nature of the artifacts and way of life of the Pilgrims.

Human paleontology

Some anthropologists are primarily interested in the physical remains of our ancestors and the biological evolution of our species. These scientists are called **human paleontologists** or physical anthropologists. All paleontologists are concerned with the recovery of the physical, skeletal remains of ancient animals. For human paleontologists, these are human remains, or those of man's earlier ancestors. Because our capacity for culture is biologically based, human paleontologists provide anthropology with information on human physical development through time and its role in the development of culture. The late Lewis S. B. Leakey was a well known human paleontologist whose fossil discoveries in East Africa have become famous throughout the world. Sometimes you hear of "archaeologists" who are digging the remains of ancient dinosaurs, or other non-human animals. These individuals are not really archaeologists but rather geologists who specialize in the field of paleontology. Because the ancient animal remains they seek are buried in the ground, they must use techniques of excavation to recover their data.

Professional and Lay Archaeologists

Most archaeologists in the United States are prehistoric archaeologists. Their primary goals are finding, recovering, interpreting and preserving the remains left by earlier societies. Anyone can be interested in archaeology and almost everyone is. The difference between the professional and lay archaeologist is that the former pursues archaeology for a living while it remains primarily a hobby to the latter. To be well qualified, all archaeologists must acquire certain technical skills, theoretical knowledge, and powers of observation to conduct good field research and to competently analyze and interpret recovered materials. One assumes that the professional will have acquired a sufficiently high degree of training and experience, primarily through a certain educational background. This does not automatically make him competent, and certainly there are lay archaeologists who have more experience and are better trained than some professionals. At the same time, just as you would not choose someone to perform your appendectomy simply because they had read a few medical books and watched the surgery on television, for those of us truly concerned with finding out about the past, it is equally disheartening to witness a site being dug by individuals who have only read about excavation, visited museums, and mounted relic collections on their living room walls. There is a role for everyone, and with a little bit of effort we can all become involved in doing archaeology and helping to preserve the prehistoric past..

REFERENCES

Deetz, James
1967   **Invitation to Archaeology.** Garden City, New Jersey: Natural History Press.

Hole, Frank & Robert F. Heizer
1965   **An Introduction to Prehistoric Archaeology.** New York: Holt Rinehart & Winston.

Chapter 2

History of Iowa Archaeology

Iowa archaeology has come of age as a discipline only in the past 50 years. To a great extent its formation here was influenced by developments in the field elsewhere in North America and in Europe. Its early history is characterized by the looting of sites, particularly burial mounds, to obtain the unusual artifacts they contained, and to support theories that were almost as extraordinary. Yet these activities must be understood within the context of the time, and with the recognition that certain premises upon which our modern discipline is based, had not yet developed. Perhaps it is more important to recognize that by and large, the earliest archaeological accomplishments in Iowa were pioneered not by professionals but laymen. Charles Keyes and Ellison Orr, two of the most influential leaders in 20th century Iowa archaeology, were neither formally trained nor educated as archaeologists.

The Moundbuilders

Archaeology began in Iowa in the latter part of the 19th century. By this time, throughout Europe and parts of North America, large collections of relics had been amassed by people interested in the past. These individuals, called **antiquarians,** were fascinated by the objects of past civilizations and peoples. European antiquarians were often interested in Greco-Roman accomplishments, or in tracing the history of their own ancestors from remote times. In North America, an interest in antiquities began as part of a more general concern with the origin of the American Indian, or other imagined peoples believed to have inhabited the continent in earlier times.

As Europeans advanced westward across North America they encountered large earthen enclosures and huge mounds, sometimes built in the shapes of animals. These became the object of much fanciful speculation. Although a few individuals, including Thomas Jefferson, suggested that these were the works of prehistoric American Indians, most people were unwilling to believe that Indians were capable of such monumental achievements. To account for these earthworks, the so-called "moundbuilder theory" was created. While there were several versions of the theory, essentially it proposed that in times past a superior race had existed in North America, a race which in some fashion or another had originated from one of the more "advanced" Old World civilizations. This race had built the mounds and had subsequently been exterminated or amalgamated by arriving Indian peoples. Demonstrating the existence and identity of these moundbuilders became the primary motive behind the archaeological explorations of most 19th century North American antiquarians.

A second area of concern was in finding traces of ancient people on this continent similar to that being discovered by this time in Europe. There, by the latter part of the 19th century it was generally recognized that crude, stone choppers found together with the bones of extinct animals, argued for a much greater antiquity of the human species than had previously been accepted. In North America, there was a search for comparable evidence which would prove that man was as old as extinct animals such as the mammoth and mastodon. Interestingly enough, eastern Iowa produced "evidence" which seemed, for a time, to confirm both the moundbuilder theory, and the contemporaneity of man and extinct elephants.

The Davenport Conspiracy

In Iowa, the moundbuilder controversy prompted the earliest archaeological work. Investigations throughout the state were primarily mound excavations. While some of the early projects resulted in useful details of mound structure and content, these were rare. The initial period in Iowa is characterized by the destructive looting of mounds to gain the exotic "treasures" they were thought to contain.

Private scientific academies, such as the Iowa Academy of Science (founded in 1874) or the Davenport Academy of Natural and Physical Sciences (founded in 1869) sponsored archaeological projects. Beginning in 1874, the Reverend Jacob Gass, a member of the Davenport Academy, recovered a series of artifacts from the Cook Farm Mounds in Davenport. In addition to artifacts which would later be placed within the Middle Woodland Hopewellian complex, Reverend Gass found some rather amazing items including slate tablets inscribed with a zodiac and various Near Eastern signs and symbols, and two platform pipes carved in the shape of elephants. These finds received much notoriety and created an international debate among scholars. If accepted as authentic, they struck at the two primary issues of antiquarian concern: (1) the tablets provided a link between the moundbuilders and Old World civilization, and (2) together with the elephant pipes, proved the existence and contemporaneity of man and extinct elephants in the New World.

Unfortunately for the Davenport Academy and its discoveries, by the 1880's, opposition to the moundbuilder theory was gaining strength. One of its strongest challenges came from the Smithsonian Institution's Bureau of Ethnology headed by John Wesley Powell. Supported by the work of Cyrus Thomas, director of archaeological explorations, the Bureau submitted strong evidence which maintained that the mounds were built by prehistoric Indians, and not by some separate mound-building race. On viewing the Davenport finds, the Bureau charged that they were fraudulent, and questioned not only the authenticity of the artifacts themselves, but the circumstances surrounding their discovery.

Over the next decade, a bitter debate developed, involving members of the Academy, the Bureau, and others both within and outside the scientific community. By the time the controversy subsided, most scholars were convinced of the fraudulent nature of the artifacts. The incident, and dispute it created, shattered the Academy. Secret testimony disclosed that the entire event was the result of a series of hoaxes and subsequent efforts to conceal them. The artifacts had been manufactured and planted, primarily to deceive Reverend Gass. Unfortunately, this evidence was largely suppressed and it was almost 50 years before the full nature of the fraud was disclosed.

It is somewhat ironic that in this case erroneous evidence was used to support an aspect of the theory that ultimately would be proved correct. Although the elephant pipes were certainly fraudulent, the contemporaneity of extinct elephants and the earliest American inhabitants would be demonstrated as the result of discoveries in the 1920's.

Defeat of the Moundbuilder Theory

Towards the close of the 19th century, the speculative nature of archaeology gradually gave way to fieldwork and publications of a higher quality than those characteristic of the early mound explorations. While mounds continued to be the focus of investigation for some time, greater attention was paid to excavation and site surveys, site mapping, and to the description and classification of artifacts. It was partially this more rigorous approach which helped to refute the moundbuilder theory.

Careful surveys and excavations in the eastern United States, particularly those of Cyrus Thomas and the Bureau of Ethnology, demonstrated that the mounds and their contents were so variable that it was untenable to suppose that a single moundbuilding race was completely responsible. Ethnohistoric data also provided a link between historic Indians and the builders of the mounds. Items recovered in excavation were the same as those being used by Native Americans at the time of European contact. The precise recording of the location of artifacts found within the mounds, also showed that European trade items were incorporated with some burials, suggesting that certain mounds had been used in a traditional way into the historic era. Further, the writings of early European explorers in the southeastern United States mentioned the use of flat-topped temple mounds by Indian peoples encountered there.

The recognition and gradual acceptance of the Indians as the builders of the mounds affected the nature of fieldwork and the direction of archaeology's development as an academic discipline. A wider variety of sites was now considered worthy of study, since, as Charles R. Keyes was later to observe, "if it is his (the Indian) past that we are studying, then not the mounds only become, but everything that our past produces becomes, the object of our quest." Consequently, because American archaeology was thus recognized as an extension of Indian studies, it continued in close alliance with anthropology, and is taught today as a subfield within that more encompassing "study of man."

The Development of the Discipline in Iowa

Iowa shared in the more exacting quality of archaeological fieldwork characteristic of the late 1900s, and contributed individuals who advanced the cause of the discipline itself. The fieldwork of Theodore Lewis (between 1881 and 1895) and Duren Ward (in the first decade of the 20th century), reflect a more systematic approach than is found in the efforts of most of their contemporaries. Lewis recorded a wide variety of sites, surveying not only a large number of mounds, but numerous earthwork enclosures and rock carvings. The work of Ward, a Universalist minister from Iowa City, exhibited an awareness and attention to detail remarkable for its day. Ward described the stratigraphy and intrusive features of a mound he excavated at Lake Okoboji, and provided a discussion of the finds and a detailed site plan and profile. His recognition of stratigraphy and intrusive features is a particularly significant achievement when it is realized that throughout most of North America stratigraphic work was neglected until after World War I. Ward was also one of the first individuals to call for an **interdisciplinary approach** to archaeology, suggesting the need for the employment of scientific specialists from other disciplines in order to fully interpret archaeological sites and their environmental context. He also stressed the importance of soil analysis and lithic source analysis of artifacts (McKusick 1975: 37).

Other individuals and private institutions continued explorations of varying quality during this period. Members of the Sioux City Academy of Science and Letters excavated sites in Plymouth County which provided data on the Mill Creek Culture. The State Historical Museum in Des Moines sponsored excavations at the Middle Woodland Boone Mound on the Des Moines River. The Davenport Museum, reorganized from the shattered Davenport Academy, conducted excavations at the Hopewellian Albany Mounds in eastern Illinois.

One of the most important contributions in the realm of research was an annotated bibliography and summary of Iowa antiquities published by Frederick Starr in 1897. This publication described the fieldwork and archaeological discoveries in Iowa to that date. While this work clearly illustrates the emphasis on mound exploration characteristic of the time (of the 244 papers listed in the bibliography, 197 deal with mounds), it also shows that data were being recovered which would provide the basis for distinguishing the major prehistoric cultures in the state. Starr outlined a more systematic approach to research and advanced the cause of anthropology as an academic discipline by teaching its first course in Iowa at Coe College in 1886.

Ward likewise urged the establishment of anthropology as an academic pursuit and supported the development of institutions which would upgrade its status. Through his efforts, the Iowa Anthropological Association was organized in 1903, and the General Assembly of the State Legislature expanded the functions of the State Historical Society to include anthropological survey. Despite his achievements however, no anthropological department was created in any of the state's institutions

13

for several decades, and the Iowa Anthropological Association itself collapsed when he left Iowa in 1907.

Iowa's Prehistoric Cultures: The Contributions of Keyes and Orr

The increase in the number of excavations across the country in the early 20th century created large collections of prehistoric materials that became the data base upon which the culture history of North America was reconstructed. Once the remains from a site had been classified and described, it was necessary to compare them with materials elsewhere to see whether similarities could be established which might indicate historical or cultural relationships. To do this, archaeologists had to discover if all finds from a site were of the same age, and then, the temporal affinity of sites over a wider and wider geographical area. Thus prehistoric research between World War I and II was characterized by the attempt to establish regional chronologies which might become the basis for outlining the culture history of North America as a whole. These goals were fostered by an increasing attention given to stratigraphic excavation and to artifact seriation.

Iowa shared in these concerns, and between 1920 and 1950, the prehistoric outline of the state, her own regional chronology, was established. Responsibility for this accomplishment is largely attributable to Charles R. Keyes and his assistant, Ellison Orr, whose work dominated Iowa archaeology throughout this period. As a result of their field investigations and publications, not only was the prehistoric outline of the state established, but archaeology found public recognition, and was accepted as a respected field of study.

Keyes, a professor of German language and literature at Cornell College, had an active interest in archaeology. This curiosity led him to examine artifact collections and sites, and to carefully record his observations. In 1920, he presented a paper at the Iowa Academy of Sciences meeting entitled "Some Materials for the Study of Iowa Archaeology." This paper summarized and evaluated the archaeological accomplishments in the state, and emphasized the future potential of Iowa antiquities. The paper came to the attention of Benjamin Shambaugh, superintendent of the State Historical Society, who arranged in 1921 for Keyes' appointment as Research Associate under the auspices of the Society and The University of Iowa. Keyes came to assume the title of Director of the State Archaeological Survey, a position he retained until his death 30 years later.

Early in his career with the Survey, Keyes prepared a bibliography and summary of available sources dealing with Iowa archaeology. In researching this publication Keyes collected all available literature on the subject and visited libraries and institutions within Iowa and surrounding states. He also consulted individual collectors and examined collections and sites in every Iowa county. As a result, in 1927, Keyes published his first outline of Iowa prehistory. In this scheme, he named four prehistoric cultures: Oneota, Mill Creek, Effigy Mound, and Glenwood. During these years he also conducted extensive historical research which aimed to demonstrate that certain early historic archaeological sites were the product of known Indian tribes.

Charles R. Keyes

Until 1934, Keyes conducted only minimal field investigations. In that year he directed the first of several field projects for the Survey, utilizing crews provided by federal programs such as the Federal Emergency Relief Administration and the Works Project Administration. His field assistant until 1939 was Ellison Orr. Orr, professionally a civil engineer, had a lifetime interest in archaeology, and was a competent surveyor and field technician, having spent the better part of his 77 years locating and recording sites near his home in northeastern Iowa. In his position with the Survey, Orr conducted surveys and excavations, sometimes devoting as much as six to eight months in the field. Orr's detailed maps, photographs, and descriptive reports, provided a substantial contribution to the data base on Iowa prehistory.

Keyes conciously promoted public awareness of archaeology. He presented lectures and published popular articles such as those which appeared in the *Palimpsest*. He described the types of sites which might be expected in Iowa, and tried to discourage the tenacious moundbuilder myth. This involvement with the public paved the way for the establishment of a state archaeological society, and the eventual acquisition of public funds for archaeology.

By the early 1940's Keyes again published an outline of five archaeological manifestations present in Iowa: Woodland, Hopewell, Oneota, Glenwood, and Mill Creek. While much of his synthesis was based on the results of the Survey, he and Orr also benefited from their contacts with contemporaries working in the state. Prominent among these were Mac-Kinley Kantor, Mildred Mott, Nestor Stiles, A. A. Christensen, Frank Van Voorhis, Paul Rowe, and Henry Field.

Ellison Orr

It is evident that Keyes and Orr participated in the techniques and methodology current to the discipline at the time. The organization of the State Archaeological Survey itself was patterned after that established by Clark Wissler and the National Research Council which funded a committee on State Archaeological Surveys. Keyes also utilized the "direct historical approach" and the Midwestern Taxonomic Method. The direct historical approach is a method of linking the cultural remains of the historic period to those of the prehistoric past. By excavating historic sites of known Indian groups and gaining some idea of their material contents, it is possible to suggest the ethnic affinity of those prehistoric sites in the same region which share similar remains. Thus the history of a known people can sometimes be extended into the prehistoric period. By the 1930's, Keyes was already suggesting that certain Oneota sites in northeastern Iowa were the historic settlements of Siouan speakers like the Ioway. The Midwestern Taxonomic Method was a scheme for the classification of archaeological remains into ever more inclusive categories on the basis of their shared similarities in cultural traits. It began with the most exclusive category, the component, which included the artifacts and features from a single site (or a single level within a stratified site). Components which shared similar complexes of artifacts and features were grouped into foci; similar foci into aspects; similar aspects into phases and so on. Although the temporal and spatial characteristics of the cultural remains were not used to classify them in this scheme, it was assumed that the remains were similar precisely because they shared some sort of historical or cultural relationship (Willey and Sabloff, 1974: 112-113).

By the time Keyes and Orr died in 1951, their efforts to popularize archaeology had been realized. The Iowa Archeological Society had been founded, and Effigy Mounds was designated a National Monument. Shortly thereafter, an archaeology program was established at The University of Iowa in Iowa City. The accomplishments of these two men justify their recognition as leaders in Iowa archaeology.

The Modern Era

The prehistoric framework elucidated by Keyes and Orr was expanded and clarified following their deaths. Responsibility for this can be attributed to the Iowa Archeological Society and its local chapters, and to the archaeology program established at The University of Iowa in 1952. Paul Beaubien and Wilfred Logan, of the National Park Service, initiated surveys and excavations in the Effigy Mounds region. Members of the Northeast Chapter of the I.A.S. participated on these projects and undertook individual research. The Central Chapter of the I.A.S., founded by R. W. Breckenridge and G. S. Guynnes, supported the work of individuals such as Paul Rowe and Donald Davis in the southwestern part of the state. The Northwest Chapter, centered around Cherokee was particularly active during the 1950's and 1960's. Guided by the Sanford Museum and its director W. D. Frankforter, members such as A. C. Thompson, Clinton Lawver, C. H. D. Smith, Nestor Stiles, Joe Beals, Roger Banks, and David Lilly, conducted fieldwork at a number of important northwestern Iowa sites.

At the same time, Reynold Ruppe, appointed to the Department of Sociology and Anthropology in 1952, together with David Stout, organized the archaeological program at The University of Iowa. Ruppe directed a number of archaeological projects over the next few years, especially in eastern Iowa, and many of his students including Adrian Anderson, Dale Henning, John Ives, Eugene Fugle, and George Cowgill subsequently became prominent archaeologists.

There was limited public funding of fieldwork in Iowa prior to 1960. Keyes' appointment had been state supported through a joint sponsorship by the State Historical Society and The University of Iowa. Ruppe had minimal support from The University of Iowa. He also received funds from the American Philosophical Foundation and the Old Gold Foundation. After its formation, the Iowa Archeological Society was an ardent supporter of many field projects, and reports of finds and excavations were published in its *Journal* and in the newsletters of the Society and its Northwest Chapter.

As the rate of site destruction increased through the years as a result of modern farming practices, the expansion of towns, and the construction of highways, the Society and The University were unable to provide sufficient support for salvage excavations. Nor was there any concerted preservation plan to protect remaining antiquities. As a result, Ruppe urged the legislature to consider the establishment of a state office which might coordinate archaeological research. Finally, in 1959, the Office of the State Archaeologist was established with Ruppe at its head. It was not until he had resigned this position, however, and left the state that the new State Archaeologist, Marshall McKusick, began to receive the support necessary to establish an archaeological program.

Throughout this period, archaeologists continued to clarify the prehistoric outline of North America. The discovery of the **radiocarbon technique** of dating finds in 1949 (a by-product of the Manhattan Project) greatly facilitated this process because it allowed archaeologists to establish more precisely the contemporaneity of prehistoric cultures and evaluate their relationships. Yet, for many archaeologists this in itself was not enough since it resulted in little more than a prehistoric chronicle. These individuals proposed that more might be accomplished with archaeological data by interpreting the function of the remains (artifacts as well as entire sites) and understanding the social and environmental context in which they occurred. From this, the prehistoric sequence might not only be described but explained in terms of cultural and social behavior. And, they believed, if the organization and development of societies at various times and places were elucidated as the result of prehistoric research, it might be possible to understand the cultural processes which have been at work throughout all human history.

To an extent, Iowa shared in these loftier pursuits. Many of the reports which appeared in the *Journal of the Iowa Archeological Society*, and the publication series of the Office of the State Archaeologist which began in 1970, included studies on the functional analysis of archaeological remains, reconstructions of past environments, and the location and distribution of prehistoric settlements.

As the discipline developed as a social science, with a more standardized and rigorous methodology and theoretical base, a gap was created between the professional and the lay archaeologist. In Iowa, this gap was reinforced as the *Journal of the Iowa Archeological Society* became more and more technical, and as fewer field projects encouraged the participation of the public. An attempt has been made to remedy this situation in the last few years through a conscious effort to improve communication between the two sectors, and to develop programs in which the lay archaeologist can take part. A campaign to increase membership in the I.A.S., the creation of an archaeological certification program and field school for amateurs, and college level correspondence courses, have sought to renew cooperation between lay and professional archaeologists.

Recent Developments

As in the past, archaeologists keep as a major goal the reconstruction of North American culture history. To the techniques of the past they have added some methods and theoretical approaches introduced during the 1960's and 70's. A few of these are new, others are borrowed from other sciences, while some represent the rejuvenated suggestions of earlier researchers cloaked in new jargon (see Willey and Sabloff, 1974 for a more complete discussion). To a greater or lesser degree Iowa has been touched by these events. This is particularly true in the application of the ecosystem model to the reconstruction of prehistory and the impact of federal environmental legislation on the documentation and preservation of sites.

Anthropologists have for some time maintained an implicit view of culture as a system, a whole composed of interrelated interacting parts. Textbooks for many years contained individual chapters on subsistence, technology, social organization, political organization, religion, and so on — essentially the subsystems of culture. Modern researchers stress that the cultural system is dynamic, ever changing, and that a change in any one subsystem results in changes to the others. More than this, they believe that if culture is the human means of adapting to the environment, we can only understand the development of culture (in the larger sense) or the workings of individual cultures, by understanding the broader environmental system of which they are a part.

In practice, this ecosystem model requires the archaeologist to gather as much information about prehistoric culture and environment as is possible. This has resulted in improved data recovery methods, particularly those related to the retrieval of environmental information. Because no one archaeologist can be master of many disciplines, it has also promoted the interdisciplinary project, which brings together specialists from many sciences, working towards common goals. The large interdisciplinary project at the Cherokee Sewer Site is a good example of the application of the ecosystem model. The cultural system at Cherokee, reconstructed by the archaeologists, was interpreted in light of the environmental system of the Little Sioux Valley re-created by the geologists, paleontologists, and paleobotanists. This resulted in a more complete understanding of the prehistoric events at the site over the 6000 year period it had been occupied.

The Cherokee project is also a good example of the increased reliance by archaeologists on a number of analytical tools such as statistics and computer analysis which have increased our capacity to quantify large amounts of data and compare and manipulate many variables at once. At Cherokee statistical procedures were used to measure the significance of the kinds and frequencies of artifact types, faunal remains, and their association with one another. The association between certain lithic and bone tool kits and specific faunal elements on all three horizons at the site, for instance, indicated that meat processing was the primary activity during each time period the site was occupied.

19

Perhaps one of the most visible examples of statistical methodology is in the expression of a radiocarbon date which does not actually represent the true date but statistically the most probable one. Thus, if you read that a particular feature from a Mill Creek site resulted in a C-14 date of A.D. 1150 ± 50 years, it means that with one standard deviation of 50 years, the chances are 2 out of 3 that the date of the feature falls between A.D. 1100 and A.D. 1200. With two standard deviations the chances are 19 out of 20 that the feature falls between A.D. 1050 and A.D. 1250.

An outstanding impact on the practice of archaeology in the United States has resulted from new federal legislation enacted beginning in the late 1960's. These laws require an environmental impact study prior to the initiation of any federal project or federally-financed project. Such a study must be made to assess the effect of the project on natural resources in the area including potentially important cultural resources. As a result, there has been a considerable increase in the number of archaeological surveys and excavations supported by the federal government or by private companies required to meet federal standards. While the program is highly prescriptive in nature, this has meant widening employment possibilities for archaeologists. More importantly, it has resulted in the salvage or protection of many archaeological sites. It has also produced increased public awareness of the nation's antiquities and the role of archaeology in their preservation.

Iowa has been exemplary in its efforts to preserve and protect prehistoric and historic antiquities. The Division of Historic Preservation is a national leader in the nomination of archaeological sites to the National Register of Historic Places, and together with the Office of the State Archaeologist, has arranged for the many ongoing cultural resources studies. The long term study of the Saylorville Reservoir by Iowa State University and the important salvage excavation at the Keller Mound Group by Luther College are only two examples of these many projects. The strong public interest in the state's cultural resources has been a major factor in drawing official attention to historically important sites and obtaining their National Register status.

The familiarity of lay archaeologists with local areas of the state has made them a valuable asset to the recognition and preservation of prehistoric sites. Local members of the Iowa Archeological Society, for instance, are frequently the first individuals contacted prior to the initiation of a cultural resources study. Their knowledge of regional sites has saved valuable field time, and their assistance on surveys and salvage excavations has proved crucial as the number of these projects has multiplied in recent years. It is also the lay archaeologist who, on occasion, has established the local public relations essential to the success of any project. The Cherokee Sewer Site admirably exemplifies the valuable role of the lay sector. Here the diverse skills of amateur and professional archaeologists provided the means to investigate an important site and the insight to aid in its interpretation.

REFERENCES

Anderson, Duane
1975   The Development of Archaeology in Iowa: An Overview. **Proceedings of the Iowa Academy of Science,** Vol. 82, pt. 2, 71-86.

Anderson, Duane & Richard Shutler
1979   The Cherokee Sewer Site (13CK405): A Summary and Assessment. **Plains Anthropological Memoir,** 14.

Mallam, R. Clark
1976   The Moundbuilders: An American Myth, **Journal of the Iowa Archeological Society,** Vol. 23: 145-175.

Mallam, R. Clark
1976   The Iowa Effigy Mound Manifestation: An Interpretive Model. Office of the State Archaeologist, **Report 9.** Iowa City.

McKusick, Marshall
1970   The Davenport Conspiracy. Office of the State Archaeologist, **Report 1.** Iowa City.

McKusick, Marshall
1975   A Perspective of Iowa Prehistory, 1841-1928. **Wisconsin Archeologist,** new series, Vol. 56 (1): 16-29.

Shutler, Richard, Duane C. Anderson **et al.**
1974   Preliminary Report of a Stratified Paleo-Indian/Archaic Site in Northwestern Iowa. **Journal of the Iowa Archeological Society,** Vol. 21.

Silverberg, Robert
1968   **Moundbuilders of Ancient America: The Archaeology of a Myth.** Greenwich, Conn.: New York Graphic Society.

Tandarich, John & Loren Horton
1976   A Memorial Bibliography of Charles R. Keyes and Ellison Orr. **Journal of the Iowa Archeological Society,** Vol. 23: 45-143.

Ward, Duren
1905   Second Yearly Meeting of the Iowa Anthropological Association. **Iowa Journal of History,** Vol. 3 (3): 442-458.
1904   Some Iowa Mounds, An Anthropological Survey, **Iowa Journal of History.** Vol. 2 (1): 34-68.

Willey, Gordon & Jeremy A. Sabloff
1974   **A History of American Archaeology.** San Francisco, Calif.: W. H. Freeman & Co.

Zimmerman, Larry
1977   Prehistoric Locational Behavior: A Computer Simulation. Office of the State Archaeologist, **Report 9,** Iowa City.

Chapter 3

Field Techniques: Survey

In the next two chapters we will look at the two primary data recovery techniques used in archaeology: survey and excavation. We hope that you will gain an appreciation for the range of skills which the archaeologist must have in order to recover, analyze, and interpret archaeological remains. At the same time, we will endeavor to demonstrate the importance of carefully examining and recording the context in which materials are found, for artifacts out of context tell us practically nothing.

Survey

The prehistoric archaeologist attempts to derive explanations about cultural continuity and change by observing and describing. Unlike the chemist or physicist whose experiments are conducted in the laboratory, archaeologists make their observations in the field through the location and study of sites. A **site** is any location where there are signs of past human activity. It might be as small as a single hearth or as large as an entire city.

While many sites are exposed accidentally through some man-made or natural disturbance of the ground, archaeologists also make deliberate searches for prehistoric and historic sites. These are called archaeological **surveys.** The survey has as its goal the locating and recording of all sites within a certain area. Prehistoric sites, like many of our natural resources, are vanishing. The expansion of cities, the construction of new roads, and intensive agriculture have taken their toll on so-called cultural resources. **Pothunters,** or people who loot archaeological sites by digging to acquire objects for their collections or to sell, have also destroyed many sites. It is imperative that we locate as many sites as possible now, so that measures may be taken to recover and preserve our cultural heritage.

Many sites are found as the result of surveys sponsored by colleges, universities, museums, and federal and state agencies. The enormous river basin surveys conducted by the Smithsonian Institution in the mid-20th century, are a good example. However, a great many other sites are discovered by the interested layman. After all, who is more familiar with an area than the people who live there? While sites are frequently found by accident, there are several initial steps one can take to help in the locating and recording of sites.

Maps

Maps are available which can suggest where sites might be found, and can aid in recording them. United States Geological Survey **topographic maps** (available through the Iowa Geological Survey, Trowbridge Hall, The University of Iowa, Iowa City, 52242), are frequently used on surveys. They illustrate the landforms of a region and show existing roads, houses, railroad lines, and fences. By examining them prior to the survey, it is sometimes possible to pinpoint locations which might have been more attractive for human settlement, such as, areas adjacent to springs or streams, sheltered bluffs, or the leeward side of hills. **County plat** books contain names of landowners, and show the location of roads and buildings. They are available at most local county courthouses.

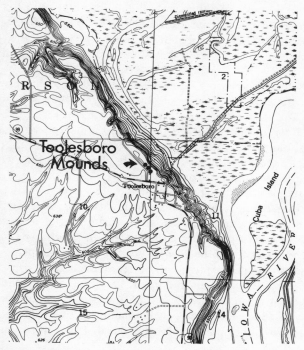

Section of USGS topographic map for Louisa County, Iowa, showing the Toolesboro Mounds.

Aerial photographs have also become useful in locating archaeological sites. They can disclose unusual features of the ground surface and distinctive vegetation patterns which sometimes denote the presence of a site. For instance, the big earthlodge village sites left by prehistoric Missouri River horticulturists frequently appear as a pattern of dark-colored pockmarks on the land surface. Once features such as these have been observed they should be relocated in the field to verify their identity. Although you may not be able to obtain aerial photographs of all areas of the state, it is wise to check with the U.S. Department of Agriculture Soil Conservation Service to see what is available.

That same agency can provide soil maps of a given region. Such maps can tell what soil types presently cover an area, whether these represent old soils or those laid down fairly recently, whether they were deposited by wind or water, and so forth. Three particularly useful sources on Iowa soils and landforms are: Oschwald et al, *Principal Soils of Iowa*; Ruhe, *Quaternary Landscapes in Iowa*; and Prior, *A Regional Guide to Iowa Landforms*. It may well be that certain kinds of Iowa sites correlate with certain types of soils. By plotting the location of sites with reference to the soils in which they are found, it may be possible to establish some of these correlations and thus predict the location of other sites. Certain deposits, such as those associated with alluvial fans, may mask the presence of deeply buried sites, as was the case at the Cherokee Sewer Site. Where features like this exist, the archaeologist must consider the possibility that sites may be buried far below the surface. Sites do not have to be ancient to be deeply buried. Some sites of the fairly recent past have been demonstrated to lie below several feet of deposition (Bettis, 1979).

Fossil soils, or paleosols, are a key to climatic conditions of the past and are reflection of former vegetation. Some paleosols buried deep below the surface may become visible to the surveyor where some natural or human action has disturbed the ground and exposed them. A dark horizontal band seen in the bank of a stream or a section of a roadcut may suggest the location of a former land surface upon which an archaeological site could be found.

Since archaeology has been an ongoing concern in this country for over a hundred years, many sites have already been located. Some of these in Iowa are recorded in various publications such as the *Iowa Journal of History and Politics, The Palimpsest,* the *Journal of the Iowa Archeological Society,* and the newsletters of the Iowa Archeological Society and its Northwest Chapter. These references could be consulted for information regarding sites in the intended survey area. In addition, site files are maintained at the Office of the State Archaeologist at The University of Iowa, Iowa City. By contacting this office it may be possible to learn of additional, previously recorded sites in the survey area.

Contacting Landowners

Landowners should always be contacted prior to the initiation of a survey. They may provide valuable information about finds they have made, and their permission must be gained before crossing private land. A bit of tact on the part of the archaeologist is recommended. Most people tend to react negatively when an unknown vehicle drives up and a stranger blurts out what sounds like a prepared speech on the virtues of the intended project and why the landowner's cooperation is necessary. It is more beneficial to take time, be courteous, and indulge in some friendly public relations. Showing an interest in what the landowner has to say about his property and his discoveries, and exchanging some information about his collection, can be of mutual benefit to both parties, and helps in establishing good relations from the beginning. Landowners should be assured that the intentions of the survey are honest, and that no fences will be broken, animals disturbed, or locked gates left open. They should be invited to accompany the survey crew if interested. Surveyors, in turn, might be wary of small, innocent-looking farm dogs.

Field Reconnaissance

Once the preliminaries are over, the actual survey can begin. It is best to have at least two people working unless the area to be examined is extremely small. The presence of two insures a second pair of hands to hold a tape when the site is to be measured, work proceeds more quickly, and it is wise for safety reasons, especially in remote areas. The surveyors walk back and forth over the ground surface looking for unusual features of the landscape such as mounds, depressions, embankments, ditches, and the like; or for the actual material remains left by the previous inhabitants. If surface vegetation is particularly dense, the surveyor will need to pay special attention to eroded banks, road cuts, or any type of disturbance which permits some idea of what may lie below the ground surface. Even ant hills and rodent burrows can furnish clues, as their inhabitants frequently bring small objects such as tiny glass beads and minute flint chips to the surface.

Survey Strategy

The progress of the survey is influenced by the goals of the project, the type of terrain which is to be covered, the dominant vegetation present, as well as time and financing. If the purpose of the survey is to record all sites in a region, and where time and finances permit this, the entire area would be inspected on foot. Ideally, this is the ultimate goal of all archaeological survey. However, where total survey is not possible, especially if project resources are limited, certain sections of the area may be sampled, the sites found then standing as a representation of the kind and range of sites potential in the entire area. In some cases, surveys are undertaken with certain problems in mind, and a search is made for specific types of sites. Deeply buried sites, for example, would be overlooked on most reconnaissance surveys; with special coring equipment, likely subsurface deposits can be surveyed.

Types of Sites

There are various types of sites. They include camps, villages, cemeteries, rockshelters, quarries, animal kills, fish weirs, traps, pitfalls, petroglyphs, pictographs, stone circles, and historic building foundations. Because some of these sites required access to specific natural resources they are found in certain physiographic settings. Fish weirs occur only where there is a running stream or river. Petroglyphs and pictographs require the presence of large boulders or cliff faces. A quarry is present only if there is an outcrop of desired stone. In the case of habitation sites, common sense can indicate the kinds of requirements our fellow humans may have desired in the location of their camp or settlement. Certain resources were as essential to prehistoric people as they are to modern folk. If we know those sections of our survey area where water, food, fuel, good shelter and arable land may have been available, it is often possible to predict that sites such as camps, villages, rockshelters, and the like will be found there. If the specific cultural preferences of prehistoric people in an area are known, we are in an even better position to locate their remains. For instance, the prehistoric Nebraska Culture houses in the Glenwood locality of southwestern Iowa tend to be situated along the ridges or in the valleys adjacent to the Missouri River and some of its tributaries. Were the purpose of our survey to locate additional Glenwood sites, these would be the locations we would be sure to investigate first.

More difficult to anticipate are the location of those sites which had religious or ceremonial significance, such as cemeteries, spirit places, and stone effigies. Again, if you have some knowledge of the preferences of the prehistoric cultures in your area, you may have some clue as to where these sites could be found. As an example, the Effigy Mounds in northeastern Iowa are generally located on prominences above the Mississippi River. We might predict the occurrence of other Effigy Mounds in similar topographic settings.

Recording Sites

Once a site has been found, it is important that it be located on a map and described on paper. This should be done in the field as it is too easy to forget essential details by the time the survey is over. A measuring tape, compass, camera, and notebook are essential, minimal items of equipment for archaeological survey. The tape allows the surveyor to measure the size of the site, although pacing off a site is an acceptable substitute. Together with the compass, the tape also makes it possible to more accurately record the distance and direction of the site with regard to more visible features of the landscape. A photograph provides a visible record of the site and its surroundings.

In most states, including Iowa, a system of site recording has been established to guide surveyors. Various categories of information are printed on a **site sheet** and the surveyor is asked to fill it out completely. This includes the location, legal description, and characteristics of the site, as well as information on the ownership of, and access to the land on which it is located. An example of the site sheet used in Iowa is provided as Appendix A of this handbook, along with instructions on how it's to be completed. This system is useful for surveyors, and permits a certain degree of standardization in site reporting. Nevertheless, it is important to gather all information possible on each site whether it is listed on the site sheet or not. For this reason, a small notebook is adequate for jotting down descriptions and locational data.

Once a site has been recorded, the information may be sent to the Office of the State Archaeologist in Iowa City. Here, the information is duplicated, the site is given a number, and the site sheet is filed in the appropriate county file. In the United States we use a tri-part system of site notation. This means that the site receives a three part notation composed of numbers and letters. The Helen Smith Site in Louisa County, for instance, is site 13LA71. The 13 stands for Iowa which is thirteenth when the contiguous United States are listed alphabetically. The letters designate the county in which the site occurs, in this case "LA" for Louisa. The last number is a specific one given to this site to distinguish it from all others in Louisa County (see Appendix A for County Abbreviation List).

Artifacts

The primary clues to the location of most archaeological sites are material remains which the surveyor observes on the ground surface. Portable remains which show signs of human manufacture or modification we call **artifacts**. At prehistoric sites in North America artifacts might include such items as **lithics** (stone artifacts), **ceramics** (pottery artifacts), as well as artifacts of bone, copper, and shell. These are items which we recognize as having been made or modified by people to serve some purpose. It may have been a practical function such as the stone projectile point used as the spearhead on a hunting weapon, or it may have been a social function, like the shell bead worn on someone's necklace as a symbol of their status. Other artifacts which we find are considered by-products of human activity. They include animal bones split and smashed as a result of butchering, waste flakes which result from the manufacture of stone tools, or a cache of quartz crystals collected for their religious meaning.

Although complete artifacts are occasionally found, the highest percentage are fragmentary. All are important because even small fragments may provide information about past human activities. In some cases, fragments tell a story of their own. Waste flakes resulting from the manufacture of stone tools, for instance, document flintknapping at a site.

Given the local environmental conditions at most sites, non-perishable artifacts are normally the only ones that survive. In some contexts such as dry caves, bogs, or in permafrost, items of leather, basketry, wood, and textile are frequently preserved. Conditions such as these are generally lacking in the Midwest.

Features

A **feature** is another important category of archaeological data. Features refer to non-portable remains and include structures, hearths, post molds, refuse and cache pits, ash lenses, and burial pits. They can also be **combinations** of artifacts and other remains which, being found together in context,have added meaning for interpreting a site. Thus, the occurrence of a group of artifacts such as stone flakes, cores, hammerstones, and an elk antler flint knapping tool together at a site would suggest the presence of an **activity area**, in this case, stone tool manufacture. The archaeologist would be able to make such an interpretation because of the location (**provenience**) of these artifacts and their proximity to one another.

TAN TRANSLUCENT QUARTZITE ●   BLACK CHALCEDONY ▲

KNIFE RIVER FLINT ○   FUSULINID CHERT △

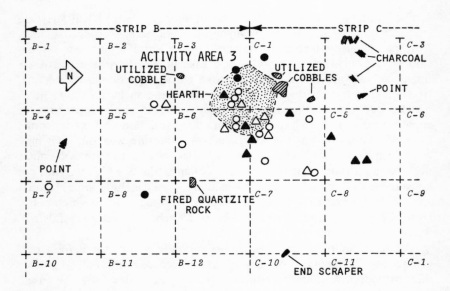

Plan of excavated one meter squares at the Cherokee Sewer Site showing an activity area centered around a hearth.

The context may also be important in determining if finds are natural or manmade. The patterns of wear or use observable on a stone artifact may indicate if it has been made and used by man, but with other finds it may be difficult to tell. Archaeologists argue among themselves as to the origin of certain finds. This is especially true of our earliest North American discoveries such as the pitted, fragmented cobbles which appear to some as crude, man-made choppers and to others as naturally bashed rocks. Sometimes it is only as a result of the context in which the find occurred that we can be fairly certain that it resulted from human activity. Were those enigmatic cobbles found lying next to a hearth amongst the broken animal bone they had been used to smash, we could conclude they were indeed artifacts.

Both artifacts and features may be found on a survey, and their presence defines the existence of an archaeological site. All artifacts, both complete and broken, are picked up during the course of the survey, but not before their location has been carefully recorded and an occasional photograph taken. This is important, for in some cases the removal of the artifacts from the surface has in effect destroyed the site. In heavily forested areas for instance where soil development is minimal, artifacts left by people thousands of years before may still be above ground. In the case of very windy areas, such as exposed blufftops and in arid regions, the soil has been blown away from around the remains, and nothing is left once the artifacts have been collected. If the location of artifacts in sites such as these is not recorded before they are removed, further interpretations about the site are limited unnecessarily.

Cataloguing and Storage of Artifacts

The artifacts found on a survey are catalogued, given an accession number, and stored until they can be studied further. In Iowa, the Office of the State Archaeologist provides facilities for the curation and storage of such materials. Many individuals over the years have donated their collections to public institutions in order to make them available for research and exhibit. Others prefer to keep them in their home where they can be studied and displayed. This is fully acceptable although we will all benefit if these finds are described, sketched, or photographed and made available for study if the need arises. Site sheets should be submitted in either case. When this information is received, the sites are given a number which the collector should then mark on the artifacts or on the containers in which they are kept. The site number becomes an important reference should the collector forget where his materials were found, or, if the collection is passed within the family or donated to a public institution at a later date. In the absence of an accession number provided by the Office of the State Archaeologist, collections from different sites should still be kept separate and labeled in such a way that their location is known.

Not every survey culminates in the location of archaeological sites. Vegetation may obscure visibility of the surface, sites may be buried too deeply to leave traces above the ground, or the competence of the surveyor may affect his ability to recognize all but the most obvious artifacts and surface features. And too, the possibility always exists that prehistoric remains have not been preserved, or are not present in the project area. When it comes to understanding prehistoric settlement patterns negative evidence is often as important to the archaeologist as positive evidence. Therefore, if an area is thoroughly surveyed and nothing is found, this information should also be recorded and the Office of the State Archaeologist notified.

REFERENCES

Anderson, Duane C. and Richard Shutler
1979   The Cherokee Sewer Site (13CK405): A Summary and Assessment. **Plains Anthropological Memoir** 14, pp. 132-139.

Bettis, E. Arthur
1979   Holocene Alluvial Fill Sequences and their Bearing on the Location and Preservation of Prehistoric Cultural Resources in Smokey Hollow Subwater Shed, Woodbury County, Iowa. Paper presented 37th **Plains Anthropological Conference**, Kansas City, Missouri, 1979.

Deetz, James
1967   **Invitation to Archaeology.** Garden City, New Jersey: Natural History Press.

Frankforter, W. D.
1953   Trinomial Site Numbering System. **Journal of the Iowa Archeological Society**, Vol. 3 (1): 3-7.

Heizer, Robert F. and John A. Graham
1967   **A Guide to Field Methods in Archaeology**. Palo Alto, Calif.: The National Press.

Hole, Frank and Robert F. Heizer
1965   **An Introduction to Prehistoric Archaeology**. New York: Holt, Rinehart, & Winston.

Oschwald, W. R., F. F. Reicken, R. I. Dideriksen, W. H. Scholtes, and F. W. Schaller
1965   Principal Soils of Iowa. **Iowa State University Dept. of Agronomy Special Report No. 42**. Ames.

Prior, Jean Cutler
1976   A Regional Guide to Landforms. **Iowa Geological Survey Educational Series 3**. Iowa City.

Ruhe, Robert V.
1969   **Quaternary Landscapes in Iowa**. Ames: Iowa State University Press.

Shutler, Richard, Duane Anderson, **et al**
1974   Preliminary Report of a Stratified Paleo-Indian/Archaic Site in
        Northwestern Iowa. **Journal of the Iowa Archeological Society**,
        Vol. 21.

Solday, Frank
1959   An Archaeological Field Manual. **Journal of the Iowa Ar-
        cheological Society**, Vol. 9 (1): 20-43.

Chapter 4

Field Techniques: Excavation

The primary technique for recovering information about human prehistory is the **excavation** of an archaeological site. The nature of the excavation, like that of the survey, is dependent upon the site itself, the time available, and funding. If time and finances are limited, the archaeologist may only sample a small portion of the site by excavating a few test pits. This is also often done at the beginning of extensive excavations in order to gain some idea of the nature of the cultural deposits, the depth of the site, and its potential extent. If time and funding are sufficient, a large-scale excavation may follow.

Goals of Excavation

Almost all archaeological research involving the excavation of a site or sites, is designed to recover data which will help to solve specific problems. Although the ultimate goal of all North American archaeology is to extend our knowledge of culture history and cultural processes through time, each project has more specifically designed goals. Sites may be excavated to recover data relating to the prehistory of particular regions, to find evidence regarding the social organization of single villages, or to discern the cultural identity and time of occupation of individual sites. Other sites may provide data which will allow the reconstruction of changes in the environment and climate over time and their effect on culture. Even in situations where a site is threatened with imminent destruction from a large building project, research is planned, with measures taken to salvage information which will allow the site to be identified, related to others in the area, and evaluated for its significance.

The diversity of problems which excavation hopes to solve influences the specific recovery methods used. If sites are known to be deeply buried, large earth-moving equipment might first be used to strip away the overburden. By contrast, a site that exists just below the surface will be carefully exposed with shovels and mason trowels. In a site where several different cultural periods are stratified, or layered, one on top of the other, the project might be directed towards the recovery of a limited sample of artifacts from each layer sufficient to describe and date the cultures present. As a result, excavation might be confined to a relatively narrow trench large enough to provide a sample from each of the strata. If a single cultural period is present, the archaeologist might want to open a wide horizontal area of the site paying particular attention to the concentrations of artifacts and features which could indicate what prehistoric activities had occurred in this location. If ceramics were useful in identifying a prehistoric culture, then measures might be taken to assure the recovery of a large sample of these remains. At another site, archaeologists might wish to reconstruct the environmental setting, in which case recovery methods would have to include those which allowed the collection of microscopic plant and animal remains. Whatever the project, the problems formulated in the research design will help determine the way the site is excavated. The archaeologist should be aware of the specific methods he will need long before the first shovel of dirt is removed from the site.

Preparing for Excavation

Prior to any actual digging, the archaeologist must make a contour map of the site, and establish a **bench mark** (also called a datum point) and a grid. A contour map provides a permanent record of how the site appeared prior to the excavation. The vertical position of all finds at the site will be related to the original contours. The bench mark is a fixed reference point (or points) chosen by the archaeologist. It might be a large boulder adjacent to the site, the end of a nearby bridge, or the top of a metal pole permanently anchored below the ground surface. It is important that the bench mark be permanent, as all horizontal and vertical measurements of finds at the site are keyed to it. At some sites, its exact location above sea level is determined, but at others it may be assigned an arbitrary elevation. The bench mark is always included on the contour map of the site as the primary point of reference.

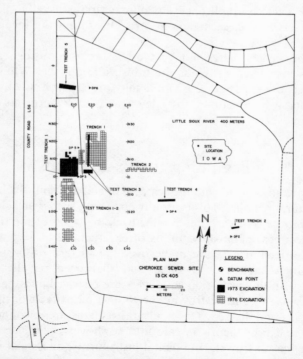

Plan of Cherokee Sewer Site showing bench mark and gridded areas.

The grid is a pattern of intersecting parallel lines usually oriented north-south/east-west, layed across a site to form a series of squares. The corners of each of the squares are staked (usually with wooden stakes) and labeled: those running north-south might be numbered, those east-west, lettered. Each square is identifiable by the conjunction of the number and letter at the corners.

The horizontal location of all finds uncovered by excavation is determined by measuring in from fixed positions on the grid, often the corners of the grid square. A nail is affixed to the top of the wooden corner stakes to allow the attachment of the measuring tapes. The tapes are stretched horizontally from two or three of these stakes to a point directly above the artifact or feature being mapped. A plumb bob is dropped from the point where the tapes intersect to just above the find, pinpointing its exact position overhead. Finds may also be mapped by stretching two tapes along the sides of the excavation unit and measuring the distance between the find to the tapes and its position on them. These measurements are recorded in the field notes, and the location of the find is plotted to scale on graph paper. Since the grid is keyed to the bench mark, at the close of the project the archaeologist will have a plan showing the exact location of all finds in the excavation.

At sites where grid units are only a meter square, a meter frame is sometimes used for plotting finds. This frame is a miniature grid, one meter square, and is divided into 100 ten centimeter units. The frame is placed over the completed square and again, the position of each find is plotted to scale on graph paper. A photograph is usually taken at this time and serves as a secondary record illustrating the location of all finds.

Both the bench mark and grid are established using engineering surveyor's instruments such as the transit and alidade. While most archaeologists are expected to be minimally proficient in the use of these instruments, it is sometimes possible on well-funded projects to employ professional surveyors.

Beginning the Excavation

All excavations begin with the removal of sod and soil which lie on top of the cultural remains. This is usually done with spades and shovels. Excavation proceeds by carefully peeling back the layers of soil to reach the cultural remains. **Skim-shoveling** is often practiced to accomplish this. Shallow horizontal cuts are made over the surface often using no. 2 spades which have been squared and sharpened on the end by a blacksmith. In this way, thin soil layers are removed and the danger of cutting too deeply and destroying the context of artifacts or the artifacts themselves, is minimized. Once cultural remains are encountered, it is necessary to expose them very carefully, so shovels are replaced by small triangular mason trowels, old dental instruments, and small brushes.

Stratigraphy

Throughout the excavation the archaeologist pays particular attention to the provenience of artifacts and features. As we have noted, provenience is as important a category of information as the finds themselves. Recovering the data **in situ** (in place or context), and recording the spatial arrangement of artifacts and features, allows inferences about prehistoric activities to be made.

Stratigraphy, or the vertical layers of natural and cultural deposits at a site, provides important information about the association of artifacts and features relative to one another in time. Materials found below others are assumed to have been deposited first and are therefore older.

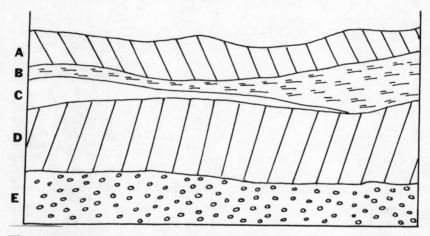

The stratigraphy shown in the profile above illustrates the law of superposition. The oldest level (E) occurs beneath progressively younger deposits at the site.

This is referred to as the **law of superposition**. Unless something has happened to disturb the natural order of deposition, archeologists expect that the youngest or most recent remains will be those first encountered.

Separate strata are distinguished by differences in color, texture, composition, and the materials they contain. If the site has recognizable stratigraphy, it is likely that it will be dug according to these natural levels. Where no visible layers are present, or until they can be discerned, the archaeologist will excavate in layers of a standard, arbitrary thickness.

Deciphering and interpreting the stratigraphy can provide the excavator with important information about the sequence of natural and cultural events at a site. Often a soil scientist may be called in to take samples, study the deposits, and help interpret the environmental and cultural conditions which produced the soils found in a site. As an example, scientists who studied the soil profiles of seven Woodland mounds in northeastern Iowa, concluded that the builders of the mounds had removed the topsoil from the ground surface prior to mound construction, since this characteristic soil layer (termed the A horizon) was

35

not encountered immediately beneath the mounds when they were excavated (Parson, 1962).

Unfortunately, most stratigraphy is not a simple matter of reading a
series of deposits as one might separate the layers of a cake. Often the
deposits are incomplete, or disturbed by rodents, or interwoven with
others making their interpretation difficult. Suppose for instance, an ancient hunter's camp was occupied at a later date by village farmers who
dug pits into the ground to store their corn. The soil they dug out was
from the earlier occupation but they piled it on top of the surface on
which they were living. Hundreds of years later, archaeologists would

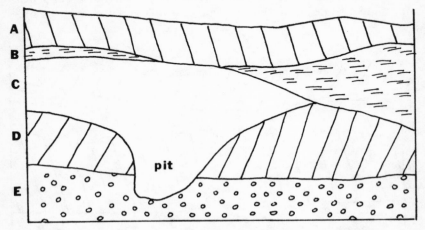

*This profile illustrates a disturbed situation. An intrusive feature (the pit from oc-
cupation C) has been dug into two older deposits (D & E) at the site.*

not only encounter this older material on top, they would find the more
recent storage pits **intruded** into the older occupation.

In some cases, a situation of complete **reversed stratigraphy** has occurred, as if someone took a layer cake and flipped it upside down. Such
a situation can be illustrated using a modern example. In recent years we
have widened our streams using large, earthmoving equipment which
removes shovels of dirt and stacks them to the side. Suppose in this process an ancient burial was cut into the redeposited over the top of a
modern county park. When archaeologists dug this site they might first
encounter skeletal remains and mortuary pottery before they came down
upon recent soda cans and plastic frisbees.

Human interference is not the only factor which disturbs the normal
sequence of archaeological events. As we've seen, rodents are a common
occupant of prehistoric sites. They are helpful to the surveyor when they
carry indications of buried sites to the surface in the process of burrow-
ing. At the same time, they are a nuisance to the excavator for they can
create a confusing tunnel system throughout a site, deposit their seed
caches, and burrow through soft hearth material moving charcoal up or
down in the site possibly causing erratic dates on materials submitted for
C-14 analysis.

Less obvious perhaps is the movement of materials upward as the result of frost heaving, and the downward displacement of certain soils and their contents due to gravitational forces. The repeated cycle of freezing and thawing of the ground can force individual articles and entire soil layers upward from their original position. Similarly, in certain fine textured soils, artifacts may depress sediments, particularly if they're wet. Where there is little vertical difference between separate cultural layers, their displacement as a result of these processes could result in the mixing of materials.

Microflora and microfauna

As the site is excavated, the dirt removed is normally screened through quarter inch wire mesh to recover materials which may have been missed by the excavator. Besides artifacts, certain types of non-artifactual data in the form of **faunal** (animal) and **floral** (plant) remains may be present. This material can provide information to reconstruct the prehistoric environment, as well as cultural practices relating to the economy of a group.

Faunal remains usually survive in the form of animal bones, teeth, and shell. Floral remains normally occur as pollen, charred wood, and charred seeds. To recover and analyze these materials, which are often microscopic in size, special measures must be taken. Usually soil samples are removed from the excavation, a careful record being made of their provenience. Some soil samples are washed through window screen, and small artifactual remains, burned and unburned bone, teeth, and snail shells are recovered as the dirt is washed away. This process is called **water screening**.

Sometimes water screening is combined with the technique of **flotation**. In its simplest form, flotation involves the placement of soil samples in water for a period of time. The lighter fraction materials float to the top where they are collected, and the residue is poured through fine mesh screen and dried, sometimes in an oven. This concentrate must then be examined under a microscope to pick out the tiny floral, faunal, and cultural data it may contain. In the past few years a number of different mechanical flotation devices have been invented, making it possible to process a larger number of samples over a shorter period of time.

In order to recover pollen, a **palynologist**, or pollen specialist, may carefully remove samples from the cleaned face of an excavation wall using a special sampling instrument. The stratigraphic position of each sample is always recorded. Since pollen is often poorly preserved in archaeological sites, the palynologist may try and locate a nearby bog or lake which might provide adequate samples. The best conditions for pollen preservation are highly acidic or anaerobic (oxygen-free) bogs. The palynologist must take care in removing the samples to insure that they are free from contamination. All instruments and containers used in collecting must be thoroughly cleaned before each sample is taken. Once removed from the sampler, the samples must be prepared in order to concentrate the pollen grains present and make them visible for identification. This involves a rather complicated and tedious laboratory procedure whereby the samples are subjected to strong solutions of various acids and bases and strained through fine screen to remove extraneous material; repeatedly washed with distilled water and alcohol and centrifuged to concentrate the pollen grains; and finally, mixed with silicone fluid or glycerin and placed on a microscopic slide for examination. By identifying the kind and frequency of the pollen species represented in the samples, it may be possible to suggest what the vegetation and hence the environment of the region was like at the time the site was occupied. If a series of samples can be acquired from a stratified site, it may be possible to construct a pollen diagram representing the changes in kinds and frequencies of plant species over time.

At the Cherokee Sewer Site, pollen collected from nearby lake and bog sediments revealed that between 8400 and 6000 years ago, significant climatic changes were underway in northwestern Iowa. The climate was becoming drier and summer temperatures were warmer than today. As a result, wooded areas shrunk and prairie plants increased. This kind of evidence helped to establish the environmental context in which to understand the human events at the site. It also helped to explain why grasseaters such as small voles as well as large bison had been present in the vicinity during this same period of time, as was suggested by the faunal remains from the early levels at the site.

When all of this micro-evidence is sorted, identified and quantified in the laboratory by other specialists such as **paleobotanists, paleontologists,** and **malacologists,** trained in the identification of plant, animal, and mollusc remains, it can be used to reconstruct the prehistoric environment. Furthermore, it provides added information about prehistoric culture. When studied along with the larger faunal remains from the site, it indicates the dietary preferences and the subsistence practices of the prehistoric inhabitants. Were they hunters and gatherers, or did they garden? What animals and plants did they prefer? The discovery of some faunal and floral evidence can even indicate the season of the year that a resource was utilized at the site. The presence of fetal bison bone at the Cherokee Sewer Site, for instance, suggested that a late winter hunt had been staged, since most bison calving occurs in the spring. When a number of scientists from different fields participate together on a project their joint effort is referred to as an **interdisciplinary study.**

Radiocarbon dating

Organic remains in the form of charred wood, bone and shell, are important in determining the age of the site. Such material can be subjected to the most familiar technique of absolute dating, the **radiocarbon method**.

Radiocarbon, or C-14, analysis can tell within a certain range of years, the probable age of organic materials, and thus, the time of occupation of the site. In removing samples for C-14 analysis, the excavator has to be careful of the possibility of contamination. Roots grown deep within a site, or rodent burrows in contact with ancient remains could result in a more recent age determination. Handling or improper storage of the sample can cause contamination. Most materials are carefully removed with a clean metal blade and stored in aluminum foil or sterile glass bottles until they can be shipped to one of the many C-14 laboratories across the country. Charcoal samples should be dried before storing to prevent the growth of mold which might result in an inaccurate date. Samples from Iowa sites frequently are processed at the facility in the Center for Climatic Research at the University of Wisconsin-Madison.

Recording

A daily record of the course of the excavation is kept by the project archaeologist. Notes must include a description of what was accomplished each day, how it was done and by whom, and what was found and where. Excavation, in effect, destroys a site, and it is only when extensive records have been kept that the site can be interpreted and the prehistoric events reconstructed.

In addition to the field director's notebook, individual records are kept by site supervisors and by crew members working on individual squares. A description must be written of each level excavated, noting the excavation procedures used (whether the layer was troweled or shoveled for instance, if all dirt was screened, etc.) and if samples were removed for any specialized study such as C-14 dating or soil analysis. Any differences in soil color, composition, and texture must be described and measured as an aid to distinguishing stratigraphy. All artifacts and features must be described and their position recorded. In rainy or dusty climates, it is wise to protect notebooks with plastic covers, and to clip pages together to prevent them from blowing away.

As artifacts are exposed, they are often left on **pedestals** of earth until the entire level has been mapped. In this way, the spatial arrangement of all remains is observable and the finds can be mapped **in situ**, and photographed. Artifacts and features are mapped to scale on graph paper, as described previously, and their depth is determined. The depth of finds is usually calculated with the use of the alidade or transit, and a **stadia rod**. One individual places the stadia rod next to the find, or on the pedestal if the artifact has been removed. A second person sights through the leveled telescope of the instrument and reads the stadia rod. This reading (the rod reading) is subtracted from the height of the instrument above the datum point which is determined at the start of each day. The result is a record of the elevation of the find relative to the datum point.

For example, suppose the datum point is 100 meters above sea level, and the leveled telescope of the transit sits one meter above it. This

13LA71

Square F

Level 6 (95.8 — 95.4 feet)
Opening elevations:

	RR	El.
N10	8.24	95.41
N20	7.86	95.79
N10/E10	8.30	95.35
N20/E10	7.96	95.69

June 3, 1976
Excavators: Zipp, Slattery, Hoyer

H.I. = 103.65

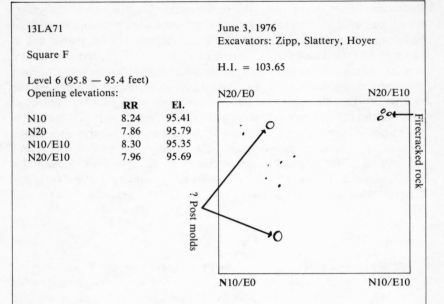

Firecracked rock, chert flakes, and a bone rib were found in conjunction with large and frequent pieces of charcoal. The latter was collected for a C-14 sample at the base of level 6. Soil was very dark with little mottling. Elevation 95.4. A photograph was taken.

Probable post holes plotted above: 4 ft. from N10   Farthest south
7.3 ft. from N20
8.8 ft. from N10   Farthest north
3.4 ft. from N20

Level 6: There were no discernible features although several possible post holes were mapped (see above). Large amounts of firecracked rock were found in the upper part, and rock, much charcoal, and bone were found in the lower part of the north-central and north-east area along the wall. The texture of the soil in the west one third of the square was noticeably of a more clay appearance denoting the subsoil level is very close to the top of level 7. Towards the east the color of the soil darkens and the texture is more sandy. Also most of the fire cracked rock was found in this area. This contrast is due to the land slope versus the artificial levels.

Closing elevations:

	RR	El.
N10	8.26	95.39
N20	8.28	95.42
N10/E10	8.23	95.37
N20/E10	8.23	95.42

Notes from field notebook Helen Smith Site

means the height of the instrument (the transit) is 101 meters above sea level. We place the stadia rod next to a projectile point we wish to map, and the person sighting through the leveled telescope of the transit gets a reading of two meters. When this figure is subtracted from the height of the instrument, the result is 99 meters which is the elevation of the projectile point above sea level. Sometimes the heights of the corner stakes of the grid are determined; the elevations of finds within each square can then be calculated by measuring down with a tape from a leveled string stretched horizontally between the stakes. The string is kept even with the help of a **line level.**

By recording the location of all finds at a site, the archaeologist can recognize any significant distribution patterns. Clusters of artifacts and features might mean the presence of specific activity areas, and could reflect aspects of prehistoric social organization. For instance, artifacts associated with women's chores might be found in one section of a house floor with those related to men's tasks on another. Thus, the physical separation of the material remains may reflect the division of labor within the household. The spatial distribution of certain remains might also indicate larger divisions within the prehistoric community. Among some historic Indian groups we know that several clans existed within the society. Each clan had its own ritual paraphernalia used by none of the other clans. This might include the possession of certain animal remains like raven or eagle wings and claws which were considered clan totems, or the painting of special designs on pottery. In some cases, clans lived in separate segments of the village. If archaeologists excavated a large site and found different material remains like these segregated within two portions of the village, they might infer that some form of social division existed in the society possibly based on the clan system.

After all finds have been described, mapped, and photographed, they're removed from the excavation. Most materials are placed in plastic, paper or cloth bags which bear a label indicating the site number, the date of recovery, the horizontal and vertical location within the excavation unit, and the names or initials of the excavator. Care is taken to protect very tiny or fragile remains in separate, more substantial containers. When objects are found broken, as is frequently the case with ceramics, all individual pieces are placed together and separated from other materials of the same provenience.

Plotting the vertical location of finds

Before the project is completed, **profiles** or **sections** of all excavation walls are drawn to scale on graph paper and photographed in order to provide a record illustrating the stratigraphic sequence at the site. The color, texture, and composition of each separate layer is indicated, and the position of remains is shown. In drawing a profile, a string is often placed horizontally across the wall, or about half way down the wall of an excavated unit. The elevation of the string is determined and recorded, and a measuring tape is stretched along it. Measurements of strata and finds visible in the profile are then taken upwards or downwards from the string and their horizontal location is determined by their position on the level tape.

It is important to reconstruct the vertical position of all remains in order to relate them to one another in time, and to document changes through time. When all of the remains at the site appear to represent one culture or cultural period, the side is said to contain a **single component**. **Multicomponent** sites represent those with the remains of two or more different cultures, or two or more different time periods present. The components might be clearly stratified or they could occur mixed within a single deposit. The stratigraphic sequence can also demonstrate the depositional history of the site. When soil scientists and geologists have interpreted this they can provide data regarding the prehistoric landscape and the environmental setting at the time of occupation.

Backfilling

At the conclusion of most archaeological excavations, the site is backfilled and restored to its original contour. On large, extensive sites, soil is usually replaced with the aid of mechanical equipment. Backfilling by hand, with shovels and wheelbarrows, is the normal procedure on smaller projects. Once the ground has been leveled, it is normally reseeded, or sodded. Sod removed at the beginning of the project can sometimes be maintained and used to landscape the site after backfilling. From the beginning to the end of the project, the permission of the site's landowner must be acquired prior to any disturbance of the property. Before leaving the field, the archaeologist must also be sure the landowner is satisfied with the restoration of the site, and the condition of any other property such as fences, gates, and crops. Adequate financial reimbursement should be offered for any crops or property disturbed as a result of excavation.

Limitations of the archaeological record

We will never possess a complete record of prehistory. There are limitations to the archaeological record resulting from the nature of the data, conditions of preservation, and the expertise of the archaeologist. Not every aspect of culture is manifest in material remains. Although we have been able to infer much about nonmaterial culture, there is much more that we will never know. One of the most elusive among nonliterate peoples is language. Without some form of writing, it is impossible to recreate the language of ancient societies. And language can be the key to understanding much about a particular culture.

The behavior patterns of the people themselves can be a limiting factor to interpretation. Highly mobile groups tended to possess fewer personal goods, and these were often made of materials which were durable to transport but which rarely survive in the archaeological record. When people began to settle in one place for longer periods, their possessions increased and were more apt to include breakable items that would have been liabilities to a mobile society. Thus, we tend to know less about the early hunters and gatherers and more about later horticulturists. Temporary structures of wood and brush, as well as hide coverings and containers of wood, leather, and basketry have long since disappeared; while the mud and wooden walls of village structures, or at least their post patterns, have survived along with the potsherds, stone, and bone artifacts found within them.

Even if all aspects of culture were represented in material remains, not every site would preserve them. Preservation conditions vary from place to place, and usually only the most durable items survive. Many soils are acidic so that organic remains including bone have disintegrated. Some sites are subject to erosion, others are obliterated by man's encroaching civilization.

The competence of the archaeologist may also limit the reconstruction of prehistory. His range of skills, education, and approach to excavation determines what is recovered and how it is interpreted. His ability to gain support for research, and his willingness to publish his results, enhance or restrict our knowledge of the past. The interdisciplinary study can compensate somewhat for the limitations of the single individual. By drawing on the skills of several specialists the chances for a successful project are greater.

Finally, many sites have been lost to the looter or **pothunter**. Just about everyone interested in archaeology appreciates the beauty and originality of prehistoric relics. But these remains are valuable in the scientific sense only because, when found in context, they extend our knowledge of human history back thousands of years before written records, and document the rich cultural heritage of Native Americans. Everyone should be given the opportunity to learn of this history and of this heritage. We can all participate in the recovery of this information by keeping a record of sites, by cataloguing artifact collections, and by taking part on supervised excavations.

REFERENCES

Anderson, Duane and Richard Shutler
1979   The Cherokee Sewer Site (13CK405): A Summary and Assessment. **Plains Anthropologist Memoir 14**.

Deetz, James
1967   **Invitation to Archaeology**. Garden City, New Jersey: Natural History Press.

Faegri, Knut and John Iverson
1964   **Textbook of Pollen Analysis**. New York: Hafner Publishing Co.

Heizer, Robert and John A. Graham
1967   **A Guide to Field Methods in Archaeology**. Palo Alto, Calif.: The National Press.

Hole, Frank and Robert F. Heizer
1965   **An Introduction to Prehistoric Archaeology**. New York: Holt, Rinehart & Winston.

Parsons, Roger B.
1962   Indian Mounds of Northeast Iowa as Soil Genesis Benchmarks. **Journal of the Iowa Archeological Society**, Vol. 12(2).

Solday, Frank
1959   An Archaeological Field Manual. **Journal of the Iowa Archeological Society**, Vol. 9 (2): 13-35.

Chapter 5

Analysis, Classification and Interpretation

Once the excavation is completed, the job of evaluating the results in order to interpret the site begins. For every day spent in the field, five to ten times as many days may be needed in the laboratory: sorting, counting, measuring, identifying and describing the remains; examining notes and maps to reconstruct the site; and writing the final report. In this chapter, we will look at some of the ways the artifactual and non-artifactual data can be handled in order to arrive at interpretations about prehistory. When you have finished you should understand the reasons for artifact classification and how archaeologists interpret the function of prehistoric artifacts. You should also be aware of how interpretations about prehistoric behavior can be derived from the mass of material evidence recovered in excavation.

Cleaning and reconstruction

Most artifacts and some non-artifactual material must be cleaned before being sorted and identified. Cleaning must be done carefully, as very fragile bone and some pottery will disintegrate when handled or washed. It is also wise to examine materials carefully before cleaning to be sure that there is no information that would be destroyed by washing. Scrubbing some stone tools, for example, might well destroy, obscure, or create usage marks.

Broken tools can often be restored. This is usually the case with lithics and ceramics. Sometimes we are fortunate enough to find all of the individual **potsherds** for instance, and can reassemble a vessel. Then the task is to fit the sherds together as one might assemble a jigsaw puzzle. A box of sand is sometimes used so that partially reconstructed pots can be placed vertically to dry after they have been glued. If the pot is incomplete, as long as there is an adequate area of the rim and shoulder present to provide some idea of the vessel's original size, diameter, and form, then the rest can be reconstructed with plaster.

On certain occasions, it may be necessary to extend the excavation into the laboratory. This happens when fragile objects are left in a block of soil at the site, and the entire block is removed and taken to the laboratory. In the case of bone, it is likely that burlap soaked in plaster of Paris will be wrapped around the find to keep it intact. Then the entire block is carefully excavated and the bone is exposed. This is a recovery technique archaeologists have borrowed from vertebrate paleontology.

Labeling

Once remains have been washed and air-dried, they should be labeled with an accession and/or catalogue number. This number serves as a reference to the site and the location in the site where the artifact was found. With this number, even if the remains should become mixed, it is always possible to determine their original provenience.

Most catalogue numbers are written in India ink on an inconspicuous part of the find; the inside surface of a potsherd, the unworked part of a lithic artifact, or the inner surface of a bone are the most appropriate locations for marking. Numbers should never be written on a spot which could provide additional information about the find. For example, the worked edges of stone tools frequently bear scars or striations resulting from their manufacture or use. Were a catalogue number placed in this location, it could hide these marks and restrict our ability to make interpretations about the production or function of the tool. Numbers should never be placed in such a way that they would detract from an object if it were placed in a display.

When the India ink dries, a fixative such as clear fingernail polish may be brushed over the number. A layer of nail polish is also applied beneath the India ink if the surface of the find is too porous to write on directly. If the find is a dark color, Artone white ultrapaque or white paint is used in place of the ink. Very tiny remains are usually kept in plastic vials which are then labeled. If it is impossible to label the finds themselves, then the boxes or containers in which they are kept should bear a record of their original provenience.

Picking and sorting

Microscopic remains recovered in water screening or flotation are normally dried and placed in petrie dishes or small flat containers. They are then examined under a microscope or illuminated magnifying glass, and sorted. Tiny seeds, snails, bone, charcoal, bits of wood, and small stone flakes are picked out with tweezers and placed in separate vials. Often a small paint brush is used to lift out these remains as a pair of tweezers could crush fragile seeds, snails, and bones. Tiny roots must be removed from charcoal samples in order to avoid contamination in C-14 analysis.

Floral and faunal evidence

Once sorted, the microflora and fauna can be identified along with the larger plant and animal remains from the site. Normally specialists in paleobotany and paleontology are required to identify the specific plants and animals present and to determine their prevalence and frequency at the site. However, over the past few years, more and more archaeologists have taken an interest in this area and have become proficient in identifying these remains.

In addition to telling the kind and quantity of animal remains present at a site, bone can reveal what parts of the animal were brought back to the camp from the kill site, how the animal was butchered, and how it was utilized for food, tools, clothing, and so forth. As we have seen, faunal and floral material can also provide information about the season of the year the site was occupied and the prehistoric environment. Such information is crucial to our understanding of prehistoric human behavior. We know that human societies made certain adaptations in response to the environments in which they lived. By knowing what these environments were like, we can see the possibilities that were available and can understand why certain choices were made. Faunal and floral evidence also tells us about the cultural preferences of prehistoric societies. We know what animals and plants were preferred, and what methods were used to process these into food, clothing, and shelter. We also learn the level of knowledge and skill prehistoric people must have had in order to acquire these resources. A hunter would have to know in some detail the habits of his prey, its location at certain times of the year, and the best way to entrap it. The gatherer or horticulturist would need to know the properties of plants, where and in what kinds of places they flourished, and how they might be harvested. Both would need the skills to utilize their products once they were acquired.

Classification

Each artifact from a site must be examined, measured, and sometimes weighed in order to describe it properly and as a basis for comparison to others. The result is usually a series of descriptive and quantitative tables appended to most archaeological reports. Based on the discovered characteristics, or **attributes** a group of artifacts share, they are placed into like-categories to allow them to be compared to similar groups from other sites. This is the process of classification. The initial categories are usually broad and simple and may center around a single trait their component artifacts have in common. Thus you might initially sort the artifacts from a site into lithic, ceramic, and bone categories based on the materials of which they are made. Artifacts which share a number of specific traits or attributes in common are said to belong to a particular **type**. Types are normally defined on the basis of a combination of shared attributes which reflect how the artifact looks (descriptive attributes), how it was manufactured, and/or how it was used (functional attributes).

Descriptive attributes could include shape, size, dimensions, color, the presence of specific design motifs and so on. Pottery types are based largely on descriptive attributes, particularly rim form and decoration. If you found a number of sherds in a site in southwestern Iowa that were characterized by a collared or braced rim, wedge-shaped in profile, with finger pinched decoration along its lower border, you would discover that this is a common ceramic type of the Nebraska Culture referred to as Beckman Pinched Rim.

Certain attributes reflect how the artifact was made. We can determine how some lithic tools were manufactured by observing such characteristics as striations, flake scars, bulbs of percussion, lines of fracture, edge angle, and conchoidal rings found on these artifacts. For ceramics, surface treatment, coiling junctures (or lack of), color, texture, character of the paste, tempering material, and hardness are important clues to manufacturing methods. In some cases it is necessary to examine an artifact microscopically or to slice a thin section from it and look at this under the microscope. Thin sectioning followed by examination under a petrographic microscope can help determine the kind of stone used in lithic artifacts and the nature of the temper used in ceramics. If the archaeologist knows the raw materials and can determine their sources, it may be possible to decide whether prehistoric people obtained their raw materials locally, or were required to trade or travel over long distances for them. The identification of obsidian artifacts from Hopewellian sites in eastern Iowa, for instance, revealed that Middle Woodland peoples had access to stone sources in the Yellowstone Park area of distant Wyoming.

Function of Artifacts

It is not possible to determine the function of all artifacts, and we will never know how some were used or the meaning that others had to the people who made them. We can sometimes infer their function by comparing them to identical or very similar items used among living peoples or those who lived at the time of historic contact. This is called **ethnographic analogy.** We know, for instance, that certain basin-shaped stone slabs were used as the base on which to crush and grind seeds and nuts because anthropologists have observed people in less industrialized countries using very similar tools in such a manner.

The function of other tools may be inferred by recreating an activity we think may have produced certain wear patterns observed on artifacts from a prehistoric context. This is a form of **experimental archaeology**. In this way archaeologists decided that the highly polished surface on certain deer mandibles had resulted from the use of the element as a sickle. When modern mandibles were used to cut weeds and rushes, a similar polish was created.

Many prehistoric tools were multifunctional. The stone mano which was sometimes used to crush nuts and seeds may just as often have been used to break open bones, pound in a stake, or throw at pesty crows and rabbits in the garden. Some artifacts were designed for one purpose and later modified to serve another, such as the broken projectile point which was reflaked to use as a hafted scraper.

The context and association of remains may provide important information regarding their function. This is another reason why it is crucial to discover and record artifacts **in situ**. The presence of a projectile point between the vertebra of a bison strongly suggests how the animal died and what function that point performed. The purpose of some very enigmatic items has been resolved because they were found in certain contexts. A well known example is the case of the wing-shaped bannerstone from Archaic sites. For many years these curious, ground and polished stone tools were posited with a variety of functions until they were uncovered alongside spearthrowers which they had apparently weighted. When specific artifacts occur consistently associated with one or the other sex in a burial context, the archaeologist can surmise whether certain tasks were considered appropriate to males or females. Although we knew from historic accounts that Native Plainswomen were usually the hide dressers in the society, it was not until the artifacts associated with a hide dressing kit — scrapers, fleshers, awls, needles — were found accompanying female burials, that this custom was confirmed for the prehistoric period as well.

By detailed examination and measurement the archaeologist can isolate and record the attributes of all artifacts at the site. When we discover that some of the attributes occur together over and over producing a recognizable kind of artifact, we say that a type exists. Thus archaeologists working at sites in the Southwest recognized a kind of projectile point characterized by a long, lanceolate shape, fine flaking, and the presence of a long flake scar running from the base to the midsection of the point. This combination of attributes led to the definition of the Clovis projectile point type. In recent years, archaeologists have used the computer to help them make their typological studies less subjective. Attributes observed on a group of stone artifacts, for instance, are submitted to the computer and it isolates those instances where several attributes combine or cluster together. When this occurs with such frequency to be more than just chance, the computer had defined a type.

Artifacts as a reflection of culture

Artifacts reflect the ideas, knowledge, and traditions of the society that produced them. Although the craftsman who made an artifact ultimately determined how it would look, that person was influenced by the standards and traditions of his culture. If you were a member of an Eskimo community, you would utilize the materials available to you in producing a winter parka. While the design of this coat would be partially determined by the function it would serve and the skins and fur acquired locally, you would most likely choose the decorative features pleasing to you and acceptable to other members of your society. Should a Sami from Finnmark visit your community, there is no question that your garments though functionally similar, would be different. Each would reflect the materials available in each area as well as the preferences of the individual craftsman and the society which created them.

Most archaeologists believe that certain artifact types they have identified represent real types purposefully created by the prehistoric artisan and recognizable by other members of his or her community. For example, at a number of Middle Missouri Tradition sites in western Iowa and eastern South Dakota, we find a high percentage of a pottery type archaeologists have named "Mitchell Modified Lip." This type is defined by the following attributes: it is hard, with a coarse to fine paste, is gray in color, subglobular in shape, has a short thickened rim, and bears cross-hatched or parallel line designs on the lip. We assume that prehistoric potters actively chose these attributes in producing this type of ceramic. Certainly they never called it Mitchell Modified Lip, but were we to describe this combination of attributes to them, they would recognize the type and might add, "Oh yes, that's the pottery we women of the Forked Stick Clan create in which to parch our green corn."

Thus, certain artifact types are assumed to be meaningful in identifying cultural and social units and in defining historic relationships between prehistoric communities and cultures. The same types found together over and over again at sites within a region suggest that these sites were related in some way. Types may serve as temporal markers suggesting the sites where they occur existed at about the same time. The material remains from sites like Colonial Williamsburg, Jamestown, and Plymouth Colony, for instance, should be more similar to each other than they would be to those of modern Pittsburgh or Des Moines. Similar types can also demonstrate historical or cultural connections between sites. Prehistoric sites which share a number of specific artifact types were likely to have been in contact with one another, and may have shared a common derivation. The presence of certain effigy pipes, Havana pottery, and Snyders points found in burial mounds in eastern Iowa, for example, revealed to archaeologists that these sites had been constructed about the same time by people who were participating in a mortuary cult shared by societies over a broad area of the eastern United States.

Some artifact types are more useful than others in demonstrating historical connections between prehistoric cultures. The more latitude the prehistoric artisan had to express cultural and personal preferences in his craft, the more culture-specific that artifact will be. For instance, ceramics are widely used in archaeology to suggest cultural and historical relationships between sites. Pottery is an artifact which is built up from raw materials and added to by the artisan. Pottery making involves a series of manufacturing and decorative steps referred to as **additive techniques**. At each step, there is a variety of processes and artistic embellishments the artisan may draw upon in creating the vessel. Although the shape and size of the pot is partially determined by its intended function, there is room for individual expression in the type of clay and temper used; the shaping and building process; the form of the rim, shoulder, body and base; the addition of handles and other appendages; and particularly in the wide variety of possible decorative treatments. This individual expression reflects not only the personal preferences of the artisan, but the artistic and cultural preferences of her society. While the individual potter ultimately chooses the attributes of the ceramics, these almost always fall within certain culturally prescribed possibilities. This is one reason why ceramic types have proven useful in defining specific cultural units and relating them to others within a given region.

Other artifact types such as projectile points show variation through time and space. For this reason they are useful in ordering prehistoric remains in a relative temporal sequence and predicting the geographical distribution of certain **assemblages**. However, lithic and bone artifacts have more limited value when trying to suggest the cultural identity and historical relationships of the societies which made and used them. Stone and bone tools result from **reductive** techniques of production. That is, the raw material is modified or altered, and reduced to produce a tool. The stone projectile point began as part of a large core or flake, and reached its finished form as the result of percussion and pressure flaking. The form of such tools was determined by specific technological attributes they had to possess in order to function adequately. For these reasons, the artisan was more limited in expressing individual or cultural preferences. The range of possible forms was more finite given the character and workability of the raw material, the intended function of the tool, how it might be hafted, and the skill of the artisan. Thus, artifacts such as projectile points were not as culturally specific as ceramics. While artisans in two widely separate areas could have designed similar looking projectile points, it is highly unlikely that ceramic vessels from the two areas would share the same combination of specific attributes.

We do know that certain lithic and bone types were invented during specific time periods and often diffused over a broad area. Thus, they can serve to place sites in a relative temporal order. However, they rarely allow us to demonstrate more specific historical relationships between sites unless they are confined within a narrow geographical region and the sites from which they come show other similarities. Even here, it must be remembered that stone and bone types continued to be made in the same way for hundreds of years.

Reconstructing the prehistoric sequence of any area begins with the identification of specific artifact types at a site, and the comparison of artifact assemblages between sites. Simply stated, those sites in any given region whose material remains closely resemble one another are assumed to be related in some way. If they share a high percentage of artifact types they probably existed about the same time period. Where close similarities occur in culturally sensitive artifacts such as pottery, a cultural relationship is suggested. Such an assumption is strengthened if other similarities can be demonstrated in house type, subsistence pattern, and the age of occupation of sites.

Archaeologists would like to be able to define a prehistoric culture on the basis of other, non-material aspects a society would have in common such as language, beliefs, and its own sense of group identity, but we have only the material remains. It is when sharp similarities in these remains can be demonstrated at a number of sites in a given geographical region that we begin to suspect the existence of prehistoric culture. If ab-

51

solute dating methods such as radiocarbon, indicate that some of these sites existed during a particular time period, then the age of other sites with similar remains can be inferred. This is a method called **cross-dating**.

If you have recorded where on the site your artifacts were found, you may be able to locate areas of concentrations of certain types. If there are sharp discrepancies between the quantity of types between one part of the site and another, this is a significant clue that cultural, temporal, or social differences can be expected at that site. Perhaps two different periods of occupation are represented. Maybe two different cultural groups occupied the site, or it could be that within a single society there were two separate clans which lived at this location. Some archaeologists will grid the surface of a site before they begin to collect artifacts. This makes it easier to keep a record of where on the site finds occurred. The quantity of artifacts collected is also important. You need to recover a sufficiently large sample before you can say what types are present and how significant they are at a site. It is not always necessary to collect all remains. Often archaeologists determine mathematically the number of examples they need to recover to provide an adequate sample given the dimensions of the site, the density of the remains and so on. If they do not have enough, their results are questionable; if they have too many, they may have wasted valuable time and money when a sample would have sufficed.

Sometimes we are able to observe changes in artifact types within a site or between sites which seem to document the passage of time. If we can order these types in a relative developmental sequence we may have a key to the chronological succession of sites in a region. Like our own automobiles, or appliances, or most material items, artifacts change through time. If you collected models of cookstoves used in America since the 1800's you would probably be able to line them up in their relative order of development from the simplest, "most primitive" wood stoves to the latest microwaves. Should someone introduce another style, say the first gas burner, you should be able to accurately place it in the sequence by comparing it to the models which immediately preceded and followed. In a similar manner certain artifact types can be ordered by noting their developmental and stylistic changes. In many cases this is from the simple to the more complex but not always. Sometimes antique forms survive and again become popular. The resurgence in popularity of wood burning stoves today is an example. Nevertheless, if the developmental sequence of artifact types can be confirmed through the discovery of their actual stratigraphic position, such types then become good chronological indicators for other sites in the region.

Stratified sites are particularly valuable in demonstrating the relative order of finds and components. Where there are clear breaks between layers, and relatively undisturbed deposits, it may be possible to establish a cultural sequence which can serve as a model for an entire region. In some cases overlapping sequences at a number of stratified sites can be linked to produce a regional guide to the culture history of an area.

When there is no stratigraphy or where it is unclear, the only way to date a site is either by relating it to a site whose age is already known (cross-dating), or, by dating material from the site itself by the radiocarbon method or some other absolute technique.

Seriation

One means of interpreting the relative order of components or sites in a region is **seriation**. Seriation is based on the principle that the frequency of certain artifact types increases as their popularity grows. At some sites we will find relatively few artifacts of certain types either because they were new or because they had become old fashioned and less desirable, while other types will be abundant because they had reached a peak of popularity. Sites which show a similarity in the kind and frequency of artifact types are assumed to be more closely related in time. This cycle of increasing popularity and then decline is expressed graphically in the form of a battleship-shaped curve. The maximum popularity of the type is represented in the wide portion of the curve.

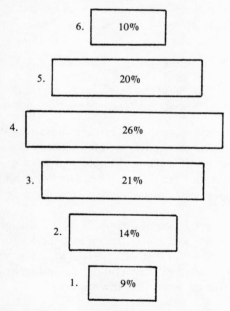

This bar graph representing the introduction, rise, and decline in popularity of this pottery type at six different sites resembles the shape of a battle-ship as viewed from above.

This same phenomena can be demonstrated using an example from our modern society. If you collected artifacts from three playground sites of 1950, 1955, and 1963 (without knowing their age of course), you would probably find a difference in the kind and abundance of certain toys. At one site you might find a high incidence of marbles, and a few

53

hula hoops. At the second, marbles might be less abundant but hula hoops would overwhelm the remains, and a few frisbees might occur. At the third, the number of marbles might still be meager, hula hoops almost gone, and frisbees on the rise. Taking the principle of the rising popularity of an item over time, you would almost certainly see that these three sites illustrate the introduction, rise in popularity, and decline of hula hoops, thus site number 2 would fall in the middle of the sequence, with the remaining two before and after. Because frisbees are absent at site number 1, but appear at site number 2, and increase at site number 3, you might order the sites with 1 as the oldest, and 3 as the most recent. On the other hand, if we reverse the order of sites 1 and 3, what we could be seeing is the decline of frisbees and the corresponding rise in popularity of marbles.

It is not always possible to determine the exact order of all sites whose remains can be seriated, but often several logical possibilities can be proposed and confirmed by further excavation and/or absolute dating techniques. Should we excavate a stratified site and find a level containing frisbees above that containing hula hoops we would know that our first proposed sequence was the correct one. This example does not address the question of differential preservation of types. Certainly marbles would be more likely to be preserved than plastic hula hoops and frisbees.

(Illus.)	Site #1	Site #2	Site #3
marbles	80%	50%	40%
hula hoops	4%	75%	1%
frisbees	0%	2%	50%

Ceramics, as we have noted, are sensitive indicators of stylistic and formal change, and lend themselves well to methods like seriation. They are often abundant at sites being durable and able to withstand the vagaries of time, thus they provide a sufficiently large sample. Styles and decorative techniques were also shared within restricted geographical areas.

If you have a large collection of potsherds from a site, group them into like-categories or types, and count the number of sherds in each type. Then compare this collection with others from your region. Do you have sites which share ceramic types? By comparing and recording this information you can begin to relate sites in your area.

Interpretation

Artifacts are useful in relating components and sites to one another within a region and may serve to document more widespread cultural contact. The prehistoric culture history of any area is reconstructed by relating finds and sites to one another in time and space, and then attempting to account for the observed relationships. Field notes, site profiles, and maps must be reviewed and studied along with the artifactual and nonartifactual data in order to reconstruct prehistoric events at each site. Methods of relative and absolute dating then help to order sites into a regional sequence.

The usefulness of these comparisons generally declines the further away sites are from one another. This is particularly true in the comparison of artifact types. Where types appear similar between distant geographical regions we have to be cautious in proposing specific historical relationships. As we have noted, artifacts of stone and bone, produced by reductive techniques, were created to serve common functions, became popular over a wide area, diffused throughout a number of cultures, and were used over long periods of time. Sometimes people in one region invented an artifact type which was already present elsewhere because it met a common need in both areas. For these reasons, stone and bone artifacts are rarely culture-specific. The sequence of projectile point types formulated for any one area of North America provides us with a relative order of the appearance and longevity of certain forms. It is also a history of technological innovation on the part of prehistoric hunters and artisans. It is less useful in demonstrating specific historical or cultural relationships between prehistoric communities.

Culturally sensitive artifacts, such as pottery, can be more informative. Here again it is the local type which has the greatest validity. Local ceramic types can provide clues to the identity of the social group which made them, its size and its relationship to others in the area. And yet, one must be careful to evaluate the total picture. It is not just the artifact type which is useful for interpreting the prehistory of the region, but the entire assemblage of artifactual and non-artifactual remains from a number of sites.

REFERENCES

Deetz, James
1967 **Invitation to Archaeology**. Garden City, New Jersey: Natural History Press.

Heizer, Robert F. & John A. Graham
1967 **A Guide to Field Methods in Archaeology**. Milbrae, Calif.: National Press.

Hole, Frank & Robert F. Heizer
1965 **An Introduction to Prehistoric Archaeology**. New York: Holt, Rinehart, & Winston.

Rowe, John R.
1961 Stratigraphy and Seriation. **American Antiquity**, Vol. 26(3); Part 1: 113-119.

Semenov, S. A.
1964 **Prehistoric Technology**. London: Cory, Adams & MacKay.

Willey, Gordon & Jeremy A. Sabloff.
1974 **A History of American Archaeology**. San Francisco, Calif.: W. H. Freeman & Co.

Chapter 6

Lithic Artifacts

Artifacts found during the course of a survey or excavation must be described and classified so they can be compared to others. In archaeology, as in any field of study, the analysis and description of artifacts has resulted in a standarized terminology or nomenclature. In the next few sections we will learn how you might describe and classify your own lithic, ceramic, and bone artifacts, and we will look at specific types found in Iowa. You will see that in most cases, types have been defined on the basis of descriptive attributes, however, the way the tool was manufactured and how it was used is sometimes implicit in the type name. Information is provided on each of the types so that you can compare them to artifacts you have collected. This may give you some idea of their possible age and cultural affiliation. The limitations of the typological method discussed in the previous chapter should always be considered when making such comparisons.

Lithic artifacts refer to stone tools found at a site. If man-made and not "manufactured" by natural processes, stone implements usually bear signs showing that they were deliberately manufactured and/or used. These signs include regular patterns of flake scars, retouched edges, the presence of a bulb of percussion, concentric rings around the bulb, a portion of the striking platform, and so on. In addition the distinctive shape of some artifacts with consistently placed symmetrical modifications such as notches, barbs, serrations, and so forth, indicate their human origin. Most signs of wear are detected microscopically in the presence of regular patterns of edge flaking, smoothing, battering, or striations. The presence of polish may also suggest that an artifact was used. In the case of some lithic finds, it is the context in which they are found which may provide the only clue as to their human association.

The following terms are those commonly used in the description of stone artifacts.

knapping: the process of manufacturing stone tools by the techniques of direct and indirect percussion flaking and pressure flaking.

cortex: the outer, often weathered surface of a rock.

striking platform: the place on or near the edge of a core or flake which is struck to remove flakes.

bulb of percussion or pressure: a pronounced bulging cone found on the ventral side of a flake, created by the force applied in detaching that flake from a core or another flake.

bulbar or flake scar: the scar left on the surface of a core or flake caused by the removal of another flake. It is the mirror image of the detached flake.

direct percussion flaking: directly hitting or striking off a flake from a core or another flake with a striking implement such as a hammerstone or piece of antler; or by knocking the core or flake against a stationary anvil.

indirect percussion flaking: detaching a flake from a core or flake by hitting an intermediary object such as an antler, piece of bone, wood, or a stone which is held between the core and the striking implement.

pressure flaking: detaching a smaller flake by applying pressure along the edge or on the surface with an implement of stone, antler, or bone.

flute: a longitudinal flake scar produced by the removal of a flake from one or both sides of another flake. Flutes often occur on Clovis and Folsom spearpoints and have been interpreted as hafting mechanisms.

basal grinding: blunting or dulling the edges or base of an artifact so that the hafting material will not be cut by a sharp edge. It also prevents injury when using the artifact in the hand.

unifacially worked: flakes removed from one side or face of an artifact.

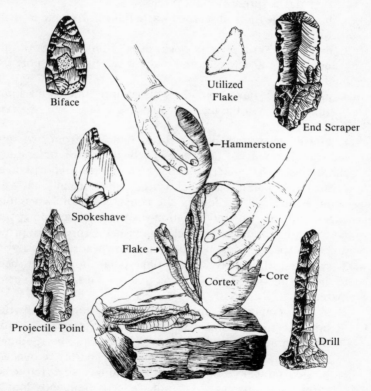

Biface

Utilized Flake

End Scraper

←Hammerstone

Spokeshave

Flake →

Cortex

←Core

Projectile Point

Drill

The removal of flakes from a core using the direct percussion technique.

bifacially worked: flakes removed from both sides or faces of an artifact.

retouch: secondary flaking on the edge of an artifact usually produced by pressure to refine its shape and create a straight, sharp, or thin edge(s).

polishing: rubbing or abrading a ground stone artifact against a coarse grained material such as sandstone to thin and polish the edge.

hafting: affixing to a wooden or bone handle or shaft using some sort of wrapping such as sinew or rawhide and/or a fixative such as pitch.

Categories of stone tools

I. **Chipped stone artifacts:** artifacts resulting from direct or indirect percussion and/or pressure flaking techniques. The materials most commonly used for chipped stone artifacts include chert (flint), quartzite, quartz, obsidian, and chalcedony.

  A. **Knapping by-products**

    1. **core:** the piece of rock from which flakes have been removed.

    2. **flake:** the smaller piece or chip struck off a core or another flake. Unmodified flakes are those showing no signs of further retouch or use. They include:

      a. **decortication flake:** a flake which bears a portion of the cortex on its dorsal (outer) surface, suggesting it was one of the first flakes (primary flakes) removed.

      b. **debitage flake:** discarded waste flake bearing no evidence of further use.

    3. **quarry blank:** a piece of rock, usually flaked on both sides to reduce its size and weight and make it easier to transport from a quarry.

    4. **preform:** a flake roughly worked into shape, marking the beginning stage in the manufacture of a biface.

  B. **Tools**

    1. **biface:** an artifact having flakes removed from two sides or faces to form a cutting edge. Through microscopic study archaeologists often determine that bifaces were used as knives.

    2. **projectile point:** a bifacial artifact which usually has a tip or point at one end created by the convergence of two retouched edges, and a hafting modification such as basal grinding, fluting, notching, or shouldering. Archaeologists interpret most projectile points as spear or dart points or as arrowheads.

    3. **scrapers:** unifacially worked flakes, flat on one side, believed to have functioned in scraping hides, skins, wood, or plant materials.

      a. **end scraper:** a scraper with its shorter edge, usually the one opposite the striking platform, steeply retouched to form a scraping edge. A "thumbnail" scraper is a short, sometimes almost rounded scraper, with one edge sharply retouched.

      b. **side scraper:** a scraper with its longer edge retouched to form a scraping edge. The other edge is frequently blunted to facilitate holding the tool without injuring the hand. A "spokeshave" is a side scraper retouched along a concave edge.

    4. **denticulate:** a flake with serrations or multiple notches on its edge.

    5. **modified flake:** a flake showing secondary flaking as result of deliberate retouch or use.

    6. **retouched flake:** a flake unifacially or bifacially worked along one or more edges.

7. **utilized flake:** a flake showing secondary flaking as a result of its use.

8. **drill:** a flake retouched to have a rounded tip suitable for boring or drilling.

9. **graver:** a flake retouched to a sharp, delicate point for cutting and engraving bone.

10. **chopper:** usually a cobble which has been bifacially worked to form a sharp edge.

Denticulate

Graver

Animal hides were scraped in the preparation of clothing.

II. Ground Stone Artifacts: Artifacts produced by pecking, abrading, and polishing of hard, fine-grained rock such as granite, quartzite, or chalcedony.

   A. **hammerstone:** a pebble or cobble which has pecking marks on its edges, resulting from its use as a striking implement.

   B. **grinding slab or metate:** a rock showing a smooth or depressed surface resulting from its having been rubbed with a mano in the crushing and pulverizing of seeds and nuts.

   C. **mano:** a handsized cobble showing a smooth or pecked surface which results from its use as a rubbing and grinding stone against a metate.

   D. **abrader:** a course grained sandstone or pumice-like rock, which bears one or a series of longitudinal grooves. Archaeologists believe some abraders were used in pairs as arrow shaft straighteners and smoothers. Other abraders were used to sharpen bone tools and grind edges on chipped stone tools.

   E. **axe:** a fine grained rock which has a sharp cutting edge created by the convergence of two pecked and ground edges.

   F. **bannerstone/boatstone:** ground stone tools of various shapes which are believed to have served primarily as weights on spear throwers.

   G. **celt:** narrow, wedge-shaped tools possibly used as adzes and axes.

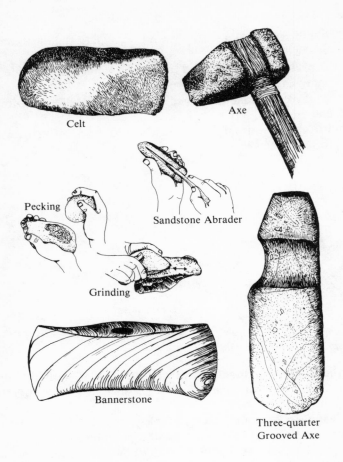

Celt

Axe

Pecking

Sandstone Abrader

Grinding

Bannerstone

Three-quarter
Grooved Axe

Projectile Points

Projectile points represent the oldest kind of artifact now known in Iowa. Differences in the shape, size, and style of projectile points reflect their function, methods of manufacture and hafting, and the nature and quality of the stone. In addition, not all artifacts that have been called projectile points were actually used as such, thus variations in "points" may also reflect their other functions as knives, scrapers, and drills.

Projectile points are not as culturally sensitive as pottery styles, although points do reflect hunting methods and these in part distinguish one culture from another. Point types do serve as relative temporal indicators, however. They have been found to vary through time and space, and this is useful in suggesting the relative age of prehistoric assemblages and in predicting their geographical distribution.

Paleo-Indian. From the beginning of the prehistoric sequence in Iowa, chipped stone points were produced by a combination of percussion and pressure flaking techniques, although the quality of workmanship varies through time, from site to site, and even within types. In general, the earliest point types are larger than the more recent ones, reflecting their use as spear and later dart tips as opposed to arrowheads. The earliest of these points belong to the Paleo-Indian period and date over 11,000 B.P. (before present). They are generally lanceolate or leaf-shaped in form and were almost certainly hafted to the end of a hand-thrust spear. Points within the Clovis and Folsom complexes were fluted providing a specialized hafting device possibly designed for the insertion of a wooden or bone foreshaft of the same width as the point. The foreshaft was probably socketed or split to receive the point, which was then fastened by binding with sinew and an adhesive such as pitch. The binding and shaft could not be too bulky for the entire complex had to penetrate the animal. The grinding of the basal and lateral edges of these points prevented the hafting material from being cut through by a sharp edge. The extent of this grinding indicates how far up the point the foreshaft and binding would have come. (Frison, 1978: 332-341)

Archaic. By 8000 B.P. in Iowa, the "atlatl" or dart thrower came into widespread use and remained popular into the Late Woodland period. It was a device which extended the throwing arm of the hunter and allowed him to project his weapon further and with greater force. In general projectile points found in Archaic complexes tend to be somewhat smaller than those of the Paleo-Indian period and are characterized by new hafting innovations possibly made necessary by the change to a narrower projectile shaft. Along with a variety of tanged and stemmed forms, a number of side-notched and corner-notched points now come into vogue, notching possibly providing a narrower area for hafting. Frequently the notches and basal edge of these types were also dulled to prevent the point from cutting through its sinew binding or splitting upon impact with the target. Again, it is likely that some sort of foreshaft was used in hafting these points to the shaft. For a hunter pursuing game over some distance, it would be far more economical to carry a number of short, expendable wooden or bone foreshafts and stone points, and only one or two retrievable spear handles. (Frison, 1978: 333-341)

Late Prehistoric. By Late Woodland times beginning ca. A.D. 800, another innovation in hunting devices had been introduced with the invention of the bow and arrow which soon replaced the earlier spear and dart. As a result, projectile point size was noticeably reduced, culminating in the very tiny, triangular-shaped "bird-points" of the Late Prehistoric/Early Historic period. While some of these may well have been used to hunt birds, they were certainly just as effective as their larger ancestral spear and dart counterparts had been in killing bison, deer, and elk.

Both the bow and arrow and the spear and dart seem to have been equally efficient as hunting weapons, but the bow and arrow had other advantages which helps to explain its overwhelming popularity. The arrowpoint is smaller, requires less stone to manufacture, and is easier to transport, as are its shafts. With the spear or dart, the hunter must position himself to deliver a straightforward, right angle thrust to his prey. On the other hand, the bow can be drawn slowly, without a quick, jerky movement whether the hunter is standing or not. The bow and arrow also has a greater range than the thrusting spear or atlatl (Frison 1978: 223-224).

Whether spear, dart, or arrowhead, the beautiful workmanship of many points documents the existence of superior flintknappers and extra effort expended on the manufacture of some specimens. This seems particularly true when the prehistoric artisan was able to acquire fine stone for his work. (Frison, 1978: 332) In some cases, he had to trade over long distances to get the Knife River flint from North Dakota, Harrison County chert from Illinois, or the obsidian from the Yellowstone area of Wyoming, which have been found in Iowa sites. The exceptional beauty of some points suggests that flintknapping specialists existed who may have been "commissioned" by other members of the society to produce fine points.

Types found in Iowa. The points described here have been found in Iowa sites. They represent types known in adjacent areas as well. In most cases they have been named after a site or geographical location where they were first discovered or where they were prevalent. The Clovis point, for example, was named for the town of Clovis, New Mexico near the site of Blackwater Draw where the point was first identified. The Durst Stemmed point type incorporates the name of the Durst Rockshelter, the site in Wisconsin where it was found, and a descriptive attribute of the type, in this case the presence of a stem.

As is the case with other stone tools, a specialized terminology has been developed to describe projectile points. As you compare points in your collection to types discussed here, remember to consider all attributes of the point, not just one or two outstanding ones. Shape, size, hafting characteristics, flaking, as well as the material the point is made of are diagnostic in determining whether the point belongs to a particular type. Points may be characterized by the following flaking patterns as reflected in the flake scars found on one or both faces of the specimen:

random flaking: a multi-directional flaking where flakes appear to have been randomly removed without apparent order.

collateral flaking: a form of horizontal, parallel flaking where broad, conchoidal flakes were removed, starting at either edge and extending to the midsection of the point producing a median ridge. The artifact is characterized by a diamond shaped cross-section.

transverse flaking: a form of horizontal, parallel flaking where narrow flakes were removed starting at either edge, producing flake scars that usually meet smoothly to form a single flake scar. The artifact is characterized by a lenticular shaped cross-section.

oblique flaking: a form of diagonal, parallel flaking where narrow flakes were removed starting at either edge, producing flake scars that usually meet smoothly to form a single flake scar. The artifact is characterized by a lenticular shaped cross-section.

The dimensions of projectile points are usually determined from standard points or landmarks on the artifact. The length is measured from tip to base; the width is taken from edge to edge at the widest point. This might be the midsection, the base, or from barb to barb. The thickness also means the maximum thickness of the point wherever this occurs. Today, almost all North American archaeologists are expressing the dimensions of artifacts in metric units.

The types here have been listed in the relative temporal order in which they have been found to occur. Should you discover similar types in your own collections, this guide may serve to provide some idea of the relative age of your point. Also note the geographical distribution of each type. By recording the location of your finds it will help us to better understand the spatial distribution of types throughout Iowa and the Midwest. We may then be able to account for this in functional, environmental, or cultural terms.

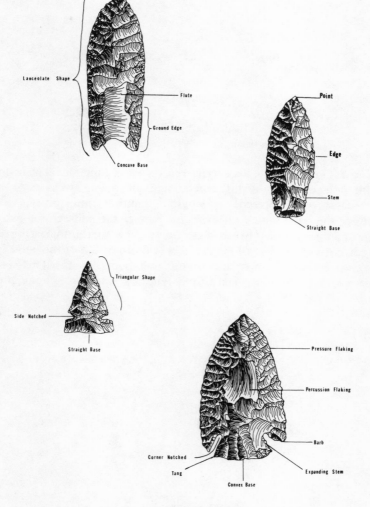

Features of projectile points

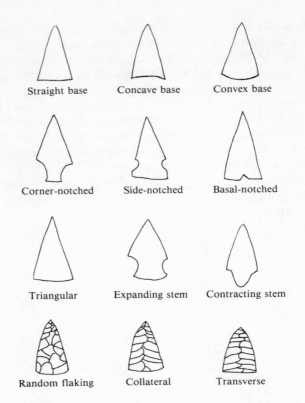

Straight base   Concave base   Convex base

Corner-notched   Side-notched   Basal-notched

Triangular   Expanding stem   Contracting stem

Random flaking   Collateral   Transverse

Clovis Type. The Clovis type represents a long, lanceolate-shaped point with parallel to slightly convex sides and a concave base. A distinctive feature is the presence of single or multiple flutes on one or both faces of the point which run from the base to the midsection. The basal edge and base frequently exhibit grinding. The length ranges from 2.5 to 15 cm. with an average of 6.5 cm. The widest portion of the point is near the midsection or toward the tip. The fluted point illustrated here is 9 cm. long and 3.3 cm. wide. The Clovis type is found throughout much of

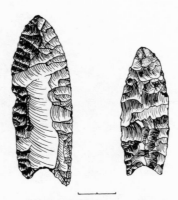

Fluted and Unfluted Clovis points from Iowa
Note: All artifact scales in this book are shown in centimeters.

North and Meso-America at Paleo-Indian sites which date over 12,000 B.P. Points have been found throughout Iowa at sites in Page, Mills, Winneshiek, Allamakee, Clayton, Cherokee, Louisa, Woodbury, Benton, Johnson, Webster, Monroe, Lyon, Wapello, and Cedar counties. These are almost exclusively surface finds, however, a cache of Clovis points was excavated from a cornfield in Cedar County in 1966. All of these points were of Burlington chert whose source lies about 40 miles southeast of the site. The points in the cache ranged in length from 6.81 to 10.7 cm., were 2.58 to 3.6 cm. in width, and .6 to .84 cm. thick. Both single and multiple flutes were present. The point illustrated here is from the Cedar County cache. (Wormington, 1957; Ritzenthaller, 1967; Anderson & Tiffany, 1972; Frison, 1978)

Folsom Type. The Folsom type is smaller than the Clovis. It is also lanceolate in shape with convex to almost straight sides, and has a concave base with ear-like projections at the basal corners. The base and

A Folsom spearpoint

basal edges are often ground. Fine delicate flaking characterizes the edges and tip. Flutes occur on both faces of the point but in this case they extend from the base to almost the tip of the point. The length of the type ranges between 2 and 7.5 cm. Most points average about 5 cm. in length. Length is generally twice the width. The point illustrated here is 4 cm. long and 2.5 cm. wide. Folsom points are distributed primarily across the western part of North America at Paleo-Indian sites dating upwards to 11,000 B.P. Points of this type have been discovered as surface finds in Mills, Cherokee, Allamakee, Louisa, and Winneshiek counties. (Wormington, 1957; Ritzenthaller, 1967; Frison, 1978)

Agate Basin. The Agate Basin type is a long, lanceolate, straight to convex sided point with a straight to convex base. Grinding is usually present along the basal edge up to ¼ to ⅓ the length of the point. The flake scars on the classic Agate Basin type are normally horizontal-parallel and the edges show fine pressure retouch. The point illustrated here, from the Cherokee Sewer Site, has random flake scars. Agate Basin points range from 5 cm. to 13 cm. in length with an average of 10 cm. Length is normally two to four times the width. The mean thickness is 3 cm. but the thickness depends on the quality of the stone. At the Agate Basin type-site in Wyoming half of the projectile points originally found

Agate Basin-like point from the Cherokee Sewer Site

were made of Knife River flint. The type is distributed throughout the western Plains and is associated with Paleo-Indian sites which date over 10,000 B.P. Agate Basin or "Agate Basin-like" points have been reported from Scott, Palo Alto, Montgomery, Crawford, Buena Vista, Lyon, and Cherokee counties in Iowa. The point from the Cherokee Sewer Site was made of gray chert with maroon streaks. It has a straight base and lacks basal grinding. It was found on Horizon III, the oldest cultural layer at the site which has been dated at 8400 B.P. The point reported from Crawford County was made of Knife River flint. (Wormington, 1957; Ritzenthaller, 1967; Frison, 1978)

Eden Type. The Eden type is a long, narrow, parallel-sided form with a straight to slightly expanding stem, and straight to convex base. The point exhibits collateral-horizontal flaking. The basal edges are frequently ground. Eden points range from 6 to 10 cm. in length. Length is 4 to 5 times the width. Eden points have been placed within the Paleo-Indian Cody complex of the Northwestern Plains and occur at sites which date

An Eden point

to 9000 B.P. It has been suggested (Wormington, 1957; Frison, 1978) that Eden points represent the narrow variant in a range of points which also includes intermediate forms such as Scottsbluff, and broader, thinner triangular blades. In Iowa, Eden points have been reported as surface finds in Allamakee, Mills, Winneshiek, Page, and Jackson Counties. (Wormington, 1957; Ritzenthaller, 1967, Frison, 1978; Perino, 1971)

Scottsbluff (Hardin Barbed derived from or equivalent to Scottsbluff subtype II, a more triangular, thinner form with a more deeply inset stem). Scottsbluff points are parallel-sided to triangular in form with a pronounced straight-sided to expanding stem, and a straight, convex, or concave base. The flaking is horizontal-parallel and the blade edges often exhibit fine secondary flaking. The basal and stem edges are usually ground. The length is similar to the Eden type. The point illustrated here from the Soldow Site in Humboldt County is 6.4 cm.long, 3 cm. wide,

Scottsbluff point from the Soldow Site (left) and a Hardin Barbed point from Jones County

and .7 cm. thick. Three such points were found on the surface at the Soldow Site. All were of chert. Two exhibited ground, concave bases. The third was a broken, reworked point which had several flake spalls removed to form a graver-like edge. The three points ranged from 4.2 to an estimated 6.5 cm. in length; 1.8 to 3 cm. in width; and .6 to .7 cm. in thickness. Four fragments of what appeared to be the tips of similar points were found low in the excavation. A tentative date of 4000 to 6000 B.P. has been suggested for the Soldow Site. The Scottsbluff and Hardin types are also known from locations in Jones, Mahaska, and Wapello counties. Scottsbluff points from the type site in Nebraska and other examples from the Northwestern Plains have been classified into two subtypes, Type I and Type II (Wormington, 1957). Type II is a more triangular and thinner bladed form and has a more deeply inset stem which creates small, sharp barbs. It is this subtype which most closely resembles the Hardin Barbed point of Illinois and Missouri. Scottsbluff points have been placed within the Paleo-Indian Cody Complex on the northwestern Plains. The Hardin Barbed/Scottsbluff type occurs at sites dating between 5000 and 9500 B.P. (Wormington, 1957; Ritzenthaller, 1967;

67

Frison, 1978; Chapman, 1975)

Meserve (Serrated version with greater basal thinning called *Dalton*). The Meserve type is a short point which is lanceolate to triangular in shape on the upper ⅔ of the body. The basal ⅓ of the point has parallel to slightly expanding sides. The base is concave to almost notched and basal thinning is prominent. Sometimes short flutes or bevels are present on both faces of the point. Those forms with serrated edges and greater

A Meserve (Dalton) point from Webster County

basal thinning have been called Dalton. The length of the point is around 4 to 7 cm. The length is generally 2 to 5 times the width. The Meserve/Dalton types have been found at sites dating between 8000 and 10,000 B.P. Meserve points have been reported from Mills, Allamakee, Louisa, Henry, Webster, Wapello, and Polk counties. Dalton forms from Mills and Jackson counties occurred as surface finds. (Wormington, 1957; Chapman, 1975; Bell, 1958)

Thebes (St. Charles Side-Notched a related ovate form with narrow, finely made notches). The Thebes type is a broad triangular barbed form with pronounced square notches. The point has an expanding stem and the base is straight to slightly concave or convex. The stem edges are usually ground. Broad, thin flaking is characteristic and edges are retouched. Thebes points range from 5 to 16 cm. in length and from 4 to 8

Two Thebes points (left) and a St. Charles Side-notched point from eastern Iowa

cm. in width. The points illustrated here are 7.5 cm. and 7.3 cm. long and 4.4 and 4 cm. wide. Thebes points in Iowa show alternate beveling on the opposing edges creating what some collectors refer to as a "spinner."

What is probably an equivalent or related type is the St. Charles side-notched point of Missouri and Illinois, and states further east and south. It is an ovate form with narrow, finely made notches. It has a narrow blade with straight or convex edges which are usually beveled. Its average length is 8 cm., ranging between 4.5 and 18 cm. The length is usually twice to four times the width. Thickness ranges from .7 to 1 cm. The base is always thinned and ground. The Thebes/St. Charles notched types occur in early Archaic contexts dating between 7,000 and 10,000 B.P. Points of this type have been reported in Louisa and Jones counties in Iowa. The point illustrated on the left is from the Archaic component at the Keystone rockshelter in Jones County, Iowa. (Chapman, 1975; Perino, 1971; Luchterhand, 1970)

Prairie Archaic. The Prairie Archaic represents a generalized type of small to meduim sized triangular to lanceolate shaped form with shallow side notches, a slightly expanding stem, earlike projections at the basal corners, and a straight to concave base. The type is widest just above the side notches. Points which might be included in this group range from 1.7 cm. to 6.3 cm. in length, 1.2 to 2.6 cm. in width, and .5 to .7 cm. in

Prairie Archaic points from Horizon I at the Cherokee Sewer Site

thickness. The type is common over a wide area of the Plains and Prairie from Canada to Mexico, and from Colorado to Ohio at sites dating between 8500 and 2500 B.P. Considerable variation occurs in this group, even in the points from the same level at a site, and more specific types within this category may be distinguished in the future. Points which might be included in the Prairie Archaic group are those from the Logan Creek Complex of Nebraska, the Hill Site in Mills County, Iowa, the Simonsen Site in Cherokee County, and the Turin Site in Monona County. Similar points occur at the Soldow Site in Humboldt County, the Lewis Central School Site in Pottowattomie County, sites in the Central and Northern Des Moines River Valley, and Horizon I at the Cherokee Sewer Site. The triangular shaped, side-notched point at Cherokee is 6.1 cm. long, 2.6 cm. wide, and .7 cm. thick. Both its notches and base are ground and it has a straight base. Two lanceolate shaped side-notched points at Cherokee have concave bases and ground notches. The base of one of the points is also ground. They are 3.2 and 3.7 cm. long, 1.2 and 1.7 cm. wide, and .5 and .7 cm. thick. The Hill Site and the lowest zone at the Logan Creek Site produced identical C-14 dates of 7,250 B.P.

Horizon I at Cherokee has been dated to 6350 B.P. Simonsen appears to be somewhat older with a C-14 date of 8430 B.P. Frison (1978: 1991) has noted a similarity between the Hawken points of the Northwestern Plains and those of the Logan Creek Complex and Simonsen Site. Hawken points are placed in the Early Archaic, dating upwards to 7000 B.P. (Frankforter, 1959; Frankforter & Agogino, 1959; Agogino & Frankforter, 1960; Frankforter, 1961; Kivett, 1962; Shutler & Anderson, *et al*, 1974; Flanders, 1977; Anderson *et al*, 1978; Frison, 1978; Anderson & Shutler, 1979)

Nebo Hill. The Nebo Hill type is a long, narrow, lanceolate point which usually has a straight base. Basal thinning and grinding are absent. Flaking is usually irregular. It is widest and thickest above the midsection. Points range from 7.5 to 15.2 cm. in length. The length is 4 to 7 times the width. Similar lanceolate points with straight to convex edges have been found along the Iowa River, the Central Des Moines River Valley, and at locations in southeastern Iowa. Nebo Hill points are found in Archaic contexts estimated to date between 8000 and 4000 B.P. (Chapman, 1975; Wormington, 1957; Shippee, 1948)

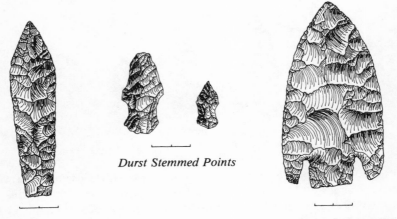

Durst Stemmed Points

A Nebo Hill point   *A Smith Basal Notched Point*

Durst Stemmed. The Durst Stemmed type is a small, lanceolate to triangular shaped dart point with shallow corner notches and an expanding stem. The basal edge is straight to convex or rounded. The shoulder is weak and side notches are usually twice as broad as wide. The point type ranges from about 2.5 to 7.5 cm. in length. Length is usually about twice the width. The points illustrated here are 4.6 and 2.8 cm. long; and 2.3 and 1.3 cm. wide. The type is found in the Upper Midwest, particularly Wisconsin, in late Archaic to Middle Woodland contexts. The type appears common in Iowa. The point shown on the left is from the Archaic occupation at the Keystone rockshelter in Jones County. (Wittry, 1959 a; Ritzenthaller, 1967; Perino, 1971)

Smith Basal Notched. The Smith Basal-Notched type is a medium to large, ovate, barbed type with straight to convex blade edges. The sides and basal edge of the stem are straight, and the base is sometimes slightly ground. Large percussion flake scars characterize the blade although some points exhibit smaller flake scars produced by retouching. Length ranges from 6 to 15 cm. and is usually 1¼ to 2 times the width. The point is widest at the barbs. Barbs are prominent and may extend to a point almost even with the base. The type is found in Archaic contexts particularly in southeast Iowa and is estimated to date between 7000 and 3000 B.P. in Iowa. (Chapman, 1975)

Osceola. The Osceola type is a long, parallel-sided form with a straight stem, square or rounded side notches, and a concave or straight base. Percussion flaking (producing large flake scars) is characteristic with secondary flaking of the edges and base. The type ranges from 7.5 to 25.3 cm. in length. The length is approximately 2 to 3 times the width of the point. The Osceola type is associated with the Archaic Old Copper Culture of the Upper Great Lakes region, and is found at sites in Wisconsin which date between 5000 and 3000 B.P. Large, side notched points resembling those of the Old Copper Culture have been found in northeastern Iowa including the Olin Site in Jones County. (Ritzenthaller, 1946, 1967; Ruppe, 1954)

An Osceola Point from the Olin Site   *A Raddatz Side-notched point*

Raddatz Side-Notched. The Raddatz Side-Notched type appears to be a smaller version of the Osceola point. It is lanceolate, with parallel to slightly convex sides, "u-shaped" notches set close to the base, and a straight or concave base. Percussion flaking is characteristic with pressure flaking of the edges. The base is usually ground. Length ranges from 3.8 to 6.4 cm.; width from 1.6 to 3.4 cm. The type is found in late Archaic to Early Woodland contexts in the Upper Midwest particularly Wisconsin, and would seem to date between 3000 and 1100 B.P. The type is one of a variety of side-notched Archaic points. What would appear to be Raddatz type points have been found at various locations in eastern Iowa including Grundy and Jackson counties (Wittry, 1959b; Ritzenthaller, 1967; Perino, 1971)

Turkey Tail. The Turkey Tail type is a large, broad, lanceolate point (or possibly a knife) with side notches and an expanding triangular shaped stem which resembles a plucked turkey's tail. The length ranges from about 10 to 20 cm. The point illustrated here is 14.5 cm. long and

6.5 cm. wide. The Turkey Tail type is found throughout the Upper Midwest and eastwards. It is associated with Red Ochre Culture sites of the Late Archaic/Early Woodland. Such sites date between 3200 and 2500 B.P. A Turkey Tail point of Knife River flint was found in the Turkey River mounds in Clayton County. Some of these points show no evidence of ever having been used. Such beautifully flaked specimens may have been considered special implements suitable as ceremonial items or burial offerings. (Ritzenthaller & Quimby, 1962; Ritzenthaller, 1967)

Waubesa Contracting Stem points

A classic Turkey Tail point from Turkey River Mounds

Waubesa Contracting Stem. The Waubesa Contracting Stem type is a triangular bladed point with a contracting stem. The shoulders are weak, the stem is rounded or irregular, and the stem edges are occasionally smoothed but not ground. Flaking is broad and flat, and the edges of the blade are retouched. The point averages between 5 and 10 cm. in length. It is widest at the shoulders. The examples illustrated here have the following dimensions:

| Length | 4.8 cm. | 8 cm. | 5.3 cm. |
| Width | 2.6 cm. | 2.9 cm. | 2.3 cm. |

Waubesa Contracting Stem points occur throughout the Midwest and have been found as far west as eastern Colorado. They range from the Late Archaic to the Middle Woodland and are associated with complexes like the Early Woodland Black Sand of Illinois and eastern Iowa, and the Middle Woodland Hopewell. Points of this type have been reported from sites in Louisa and Jones counties. The two points illustrated on the left are from Jones County sites. (Baerreis, 1953; Ritzenthaller, 1967; Perino, 1971)

Snyders Type. The Snyders type is a broad, triangular form with deep corner notches and an expanding convex base. It ranges in length from about 6.4 to 15.3 cm. The examples illustrated here have the following dimensions:

Length	6.9 cm.	8 cm.	6.7 cm.
Width	4.7 cm.	4.6 cm.	4.5 cm.

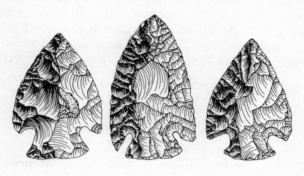

Typical Snyders projectile points

The Snyders point consistently occurs in Middle Woodland Hopewellian contexts distributed throughout the midwestern and eastern United States. Such sites date between 2500 and 1500 B.P. Snyders points occur at sites in Iowa especially the Hopewellian mound sites in the eastern part of the state. (Bell, 1958; Ritzenthaller, 1967)

Unnotched Triangular Points. Small, simple, triangular-shaped points with generally straight or concave bases, and occasionally serrated edges occur in late Prehistoric sites over much of the eastern United States. Most of these points range from 2 to 4 cm. in length. They are found in Late Woodland sites and become the primary point type at Mississippian sites. Among the Late Prehistoric cultures of Iowa they are the predominate type in Oneota contexts. They date from about A.D. 800 into early historic times. (Ritzenthaller, 1967; Bell, 1960)

Unnotched triangular point common to Late Prehistoric sites

A Plains side-notched point

Triangular, Side-Notched. A variety of small, triangular, side-notched points with square bases appear at sites across North America beginning about A.D. 1000 and continuing into the historic period. These points are sharply angled and have notches which range from acutely "u-shaped" to almost square. Frequently a centrally placed basal notch is also present. A number of regional types and varieties have been defined throughout the Midwest. Iowa points within this category include those reminiscent of the Cahokia point of the Mississippi Valley (Barrett, 1933 and Ritzenthaller, 1967) as well as points like the one illustrated here, which appear similar to the Plains Side-notched category of the Central and Northwestern Plains area (Kehoe, 1966 and 1973). Many of these side-notched points, as well as the small, unnotched triangular form described above, were true arrowheads, not spear or dart points. Such points are commonly found in Late Prehistoric Iowa contexts among Late Woodland, Great Oasis, Glenwood, and Mill Creek cultures. (Ritzenthaller, 1967; Barrett, 1933; Kehoe, 1966, 1973; Frison, 1978)

REFERENCES

Agogino, George and W. D. Frankforter
1960 A Paleo-Indian Bison Kill in Northwest Iowa. **American Antiquity,** Vol. 25: 414-415.

Anderson, Adrian and Joseph A. Tiffany
1972 Rummels-Maske: A Clovis Find Spot in Iowa. **Plains Anthropologist,** Vol. 17: 55-59.

Anderson, Duane **et al**
1978 The Lewis Central School Site (13PW5): A Resolution of Ideological Conflicts at an Archaic Ossuary in Western Iowa. **Plains Anthropologist,** Vol. 23 (81): 183-219.

Anderson, Duane C. and Richard Shutler, Jr.
1979 The Cherokee Sewer Site (13CK405): A Summary and Assessment. **Plains Anthropologist Memoir 14.**

Baerreis, David A.
1953 Blackhawk Village Site. **Journal of the Iowa Archeological Society,** Vol. 2 (4): 5-20.

Barrett, S. A.
1933 Ancient Aztalan. **Milwaukee Public Museum Bulletin, No. 13.**

Bell, Robert E.
1958 Guide to the Identification of Certain American Indian Projectile Points. **Oklahoma Anthropological Society, Special Bulletin 1.**
1960 Guide to the Identification of Certain American Indian Projectile Points. **Oklahoma Anthropological Society, Special Bulletin 2.**

Chapman, Carl H.
1975 **The Archaeology of Missouri, 1.** Columbia: University of Missouri Press.

Crabtree, Don.
1972 An Introduction to Flintworking. **Occasional Papers of the Idaho State University Museum, 28.**

Flanders, Richard
1977   The Soldow Site: An Archaic Component from North Central Iowa: **Journal of the Iowa Archeological Society,** Vol. 10 (4): 26-31.

Frankforter, W. D.
1959   A Preceramic Site in Western Iowa. **Journal of the Iowa Archeological Society,** Vol. 8 (4): 47-72.
1961   Meaning of the Archaic and Possible Relationships. **Journal of the Iowa Archeological Society,** Vol. 10 (4): 26-31.

Frankforter, W. D. and George A. Agogino
1959   Archaic and Paleo-Indian Archaeological Discoveries in Western Iowan. **Texas Journal of Science,** Vol. 11 (4): 482-491.
1960   The Simonsen Site: Report for the Summer of 1959. **Plains Anthropologist,** Vol. 5 (10): 65-70.

Frison, George
1978   **Prehistoric Hunters of the High Plains.** New York: Academic Press.

Kehoe, Thomas F.
1966   The small, sidenotched point system of the Northern Plains. **American Antiquity,** Vol. 31 (6): 827-841.
1973   The Gull Lake Site: A Prehistoric Bison Drive Site in Southwestern Saskatchewan. **Milwaukee Museum Publications in Anthropology and History, No. 1.**

Luchterhand, Kubet
1970   Early Archaic Projectile Points. **Illinois Archaeological Survey Monograph 2.**

Perino, Gregory
1968   Guide to the Identification of Certain American Indian Projectile Points. **Special Bulletin of the Oklahoma Anthropological Society, No. 3.**

Perino, Gregory
1971   Guide to the Identification of Certain American Indian Projectile Points. **Special Bulletin of the Oklahoma Anthropological Society, No. 4.**

Kivett, Marvin F.
1962   Logan Creek Complex. Copy of paper presented at 20th **Plains Anthropological Conference** at Lincoln, Nebraska, 1962.
1938   Notes and News, **American Antiquity,** Vol. 23: 337.

Ritzenthaller, Robert
1946   The Osceola Site. **Wisconsin Archeologist,** Vol. 27 (3): 53-70.
1967   A Guide to Wisconsin Indian Projectile Point Types. **Milwaukee Public Museum Popular Science Series, 11.**

Ritzenthaller, Robert and George J. Quimby
1962   The Red Ochre Culture of the Upper Great Lakes and Adjacent Areas. **Chicago Natural History Museum Fieldiana: Anthropology,** Vol. 36 (11).

Ruppe, Reynold
1954   An Archaic Site at Olin, Iowa. **Journal of the Iowa Archeological Society,** Vol. 3 (4): 12-15.

Shippee, J. M.
1948   Nebo Hill, A Lithic Complex in Western Missouri. **American Antiquity,** Vol. 14 (1): 29-32.

Shutler, Richard and Duane Anderson **et al.**
1974   Preliminary Report of a Stratified Paleo-Indian/Archaic Site in Northwestern Iowa. **Journal of the Iowa Archeological Society,** Vol. 21.

South Dakota Archaeological Research Center
n.d.   Cataloging Guide to Lithic Artifacts. Ft. Meade.

Whiteford, Andrew Hunter
1970   **North American Indian Arts.** New York: Golden Press.

Wittry, Warren
1959a Archeological Studies of Four Wisconsin Rockshelters. **Wisconsin Archeologist,** Vol. 40 (4): 37-267.
1959b The Raddatz Rockshelter, Wisconsin. **Wisconsin Archeologist,** Vol. 40 (2): 33-69.

Wormington, H. Marie
1957   Ancient Man in North America. **Denver Museum of Natural History Popular Series, 4.**

In addition, almost every issue of the newsletters of the Iowa Archeological Society and its Northwest Chapter, as well as other issues of the **Journal of the Iowa Archeological Society** not cited here, contain information on stone artifacts found in Iowa.

Chapter 7

Ceramic Artifacts

Ceramic artifacts are those made out of fired clay. When we speak of ceramics, pottery vessels are usually implied, but other ceramic artifacts include pipes, figurines, beads and gaming pieces. Ceramics most commonly occur as potsherds, or simply sherds (sometimes spelled shards), the fragmentary pieces or remains of broken pottery. Occasionally, whole pots have been found but this is the exception. The breakable, yet durable nature of ceramics means that they have survived in abundance at many archaeological sites. Ceramics are also highly variable in form and decoration. Prehistoric pottery making involved a series of steps. At each point in the process there was wide latitude in the materials, techniques, and decoration the potter might use. This permitted endless opportunities for artistic, cultural, and individual expression. Each culture made distinctive types of pottery, and often we are able to identify a prehistoric culture and trace its relationship to other cultures on the basis of ceramics.

Ceramics also reflect social differentiation within a prehistoric society. Differences in mortuary pottery for instance, where elaborate, well-made pottery was placed in some graves, and ordinary, less lavish ware accompanied other individuals, suggest status differentiation within the society. The continuation of certain styles and designs over what appear to be several generations indicates the existence of social mechanisms working to maintain certain ceramic traditions. One of the most apparent is a matrilocal situation where women learned the art of pottery making from their mothers and female relatives with whom they continued to live after marriage. In this way, the favorite family designs were passed down through succeeding generations within the same community.

Favorite ceramic styles and designs often diffused throughout prehistoric communities. Actual trade ware was exchanged from one group to another. As a result, ceramics can provide clues regarding prehistoric contact and trade.

Pottery making

The quality of the clay used in pottery making varied from region to region. Sometimes considerable effort was expended in acquiring clay from favorite sources. Over the past few years, archaeologists have attempted to identify the source of clay incorporated into local ceramics. This information can suggest how far a potter had to travel for clay supplies, and whether or not trade might have been involved.

Once acquired, the clay had to be cleaned. It may have been dried and powdered which made it more convenient to store. When ready to use, the potter added temper and water to the clay and kneaded it like dough.

Kneading helps remove air pockets which can expand in firing, causing a pot to explode. Kneading also evens the consistency of the paste and improves plasticity. Temper is an ingredient which prevents the vessel from cracking during the drying and firing process as the clay expands. Temper reduces shrinkage, permits fairly rapid firing, and keeps the clay porous, thus allowing for some unevenness of temperature (Riegger, 1972: 20-26). Prehistoric temper was made of grass or plant fiber; sand; or crushed stone, bone, shell, and other potsherds (referred to as grog).

Sometimes a certain temper was favored by the potters in a particular culture. This trait may help the prehistorian identify the ceramic remains of that culture. The Late Prehistoric Oneota culture in Iowa, for instance, preferred the use of burned and crushed shell temper for pottery making.

Once the clay was prepared, the potter was ready to make a vessel. In prehistoric North America, coiling, lump modeling, and molding, or a combination of these, were apparently the three primary techniques of pottery making (Shepard, 1965: 65). While prehistoric potters in the Old World used the potter's wheel this device was absent among New World societies, although Yucatecan potters used a cylindrical wooden disc called a "kabal" on which to form and shape their pots. Some archaeologists have referred to this device as a primitive potter's wheel (Shepard, 1965: 61).

In coiling, the potter rolled a piece of clay into a coil which was fastened to a prepared clay base. The base might be supported inside the bottom of another pot, a basket, a hollow in the ground, or in some other shallow container. The vessel walls were built up by laying on additional coils. Each coiled layer was welded to the layer beneath it by pinching. The vessel walls were subsequently thinned and smoothed by scraping with an object such as a shell or potsherd. Sometimes a wooden paddle was used to beat the exterior walls while supporting the vessel from the inside with an anvil stone. This process served to further bond the coils, thin the walls, and shape the vessel (Shepard, 1965: 59).

In modeling, a lump of clay was worked — hollowed, squeezed, patted, pulled, and so on — into the general vessel form and further shaped and refined using the paddle and anvil technique. Sometimes vessels were created using the methods of both modeling and coiling (Shepard, 1965: 55-57).

Molding, or pressing the clay into a form, seems to have had a more limited distribution among aboriginal American potters. It was employed, particularly as a decorative technique, in Peru and Mexico (Shepard, 1965: 54, 63-65).

Paddles used in ceramic making were sometimes wrapped with cordage. It may be that a plain piece of wood became damp from the clay and tended to stick to the vessel walls. Cord wrapping may have prevented this.

The surface of a vessel might be finished by smoothing and polishing. The vessel was moistened with water and an object such as a pebble or

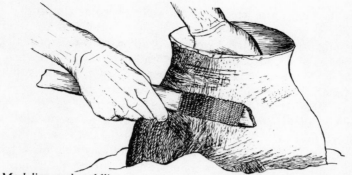

Modeling and paddling were two techniques used in pottery making

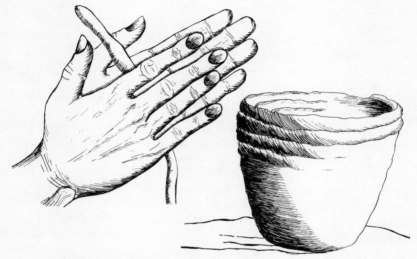

Prehistoric pottery in Iowa was sometimes made by coiling

corn cob was rubbed and scraped over its surface. The pot could be polished before it dried by rubbing its damp surface with a smooth stone or a spatulate shaped bone tool.

Decoration

In Iowa, almost all ceramic decoration was of the type applied before firing. This commonly took the form of incising and stamping (or impressing). Incised designs (as the term is used by Shepard, 1965) represent those scratched, cut, grooved, or dragged into the vessel surface using pointed objects of varying degrees of sharpness such as a wooden stick, a bone awl, a stone flake, or a sharp-edged bone knife. Ives (1962) and Henning (1969) use the term incising in a more restrictive sense with reference to Mill Creek ceramics. The nature of the incised line was influenced by the dryness of the vessel paste. Very wet clay responded differently than did paste which was allowed to become almost dry.

A variety of decorative impressions were produced by stamping. Stamps might include carved wooden paddles, cord-wrapped sticks, or single pieces of cordage. Stamped decoration might also be created by impressing the vessel surface with the potter's fingernails, rolling the edge of a notched tool across the surface (dentate stamping), or walking a shell or other curved-edged object back and forth across the wet paste (rocker stamping). On Late Woodland ceramics, a woven fabric collar was placed over the rim and shoulder area of the pot leaving the woven fabric design impressed on the surface. Punctations were made by poking the unfired vessel with a blunt-ended tool or the finger. This sometimes caused the clay to be pushed outward on the opposite surface creating raised bumps, referred to as bosses. Applique nodes might also be produced by adding small lumps of clay to the vessel surface.

Decorative and functional additions such as handles and lugs, or human and animal effigies which also sometimes served as handles, were modeled by hand and welded to the vessel. These same features might also be produced by working the surface of the vessel itself. In some parts of North America, these additions were created in a mold and added to the pot, however, molding has not been demonstrated as a technique used in prehistoric Iowa ceramics. The vessel surface might also be manipulated to produce other decorative effects. Thus, by pinching the lip, a fluted design was created on the rim of some Late Prehistoric vessels. At Nebraska Culture sites at Glenwood, clay collars were created on the rim of many vessels by doubling the rim back on itself, or by adding wide strips of clay to the outer rim surface.

Slipping is a decorative treatment found on some Late Prehistoric Iowa vessels. A slip is a liquid wash composed of colored clay and water which fills the pores in the paste and creates a smooth, evenly colored surface. Once a slip has dried, it can also be polished by rubbing.

Paint, made from various plants and ground mineral pigments such as iron oxide (hematite), also occurs on some prehistoric Iowa vessels. Such paint was probably applied with a brush, frayed stick, or a cancellous piece of bone.

Rarely do we find engraved designs on prehistoric Iowa pottery. Engraving is a term used by most archaeologists to describe incised decoration which was applied to a vessel surface after the pot was fired.

Firing

Prehistoric ceramic makers in Iowa presumably fired their vessels in the open. The pots may have been raised slightly above the ground on rocks or perhaps a combination of rocks and branches, allowing the air and heat to circulate around them. Some experience was required here in order to avoid using rocks, such as limestone, which might explode during firing.

Large quantities of fuel had to be collected prior to firing. Various sorts of materials including wood, bark, brush, grass, animal dung, and perhaps peat and lignite may have been used as fuel by prehistoric Iowa potters. Again, some familiarity with the properties of these various fuels was essential as some burn more quickly than others, produce a hotter flame, or cause considerable smoke, thus creating different results in the final product. Various firing methods were probably employed depending upon the type of fuel used and the desired results. Pottery might be covered with fuel for instance and then fired, or placed in preheated materials, sometimes in fuel which had burned to the ash stage.

Temperature played an important role in the firing process. Native Iowa pottery was fairly soft as the result of low firing temperature. Seldom would the temperature of the fire have achieved 1800 degrees F. The amount of air which circulated also affected the final outcome. Where more air was present, oxygen combined with iron in the clay, producing a red color on the pottery. When the amount of oxygen was reduced, the iron combined with other elements resulting in dark gray to black colored vessels. Imperfectly fired pottery is unevenly colored with smudges or areas of discoloration sometimes referred to as firing clouds. The potter may have manipulated the amount of oxygen in the fire to produce an atmosphere of oxidation or reduction in order to create desired colors in the finished vessels.

Ceramics in Iowa

On the following outline, the attributes commonly used in ceramic analysis and classification are defined, and an attempt has been made to help you recognize them on pottery found in your local area. For those interested in pursuing the subjects of pottery making and ceramic analysis in more detail, Anna Shepard's 1965 publication *Ceramics for the Archaeologist* is strongly recommended.

The discussion of prehistoric Iowa ceramics which concludes this chapter, should help you to identify pottery in your own collections and relate it culturally and temporally to that found elsewhere in Iowa. References to more detailed descriptions of Iowa types are also provided.

CERAMIC ATTRIBUTES (Based on R. Wheeler, 1952; A. Shepard, 1965)
A. Method of Manufacture: how the vessel was made.
　1. Coiling: May be detected by the presence of horizontal coil junctures visible in the cross-section of a sherd. Paddling was sometimes used to refine the shape of the coiled pot.
　2. Modeling and paddling: Modeling is assumed to have been the manufacturing method used if the vessel is characterized by the following:
　　a. absence of coil junctures.
　　b. presence of thicker shoulder and rim sherds relative to body sherds (ie. the body of the pot was paddled thinner).
　　c. tendency of the sherds to split down the center dividing into in-

terior and exterior portions.

    d. presence of the following surface treatments:

        (1) cord marking or cord roughening: cord impressions left as linear marks (horizontal, vertical, crisscrossed) on the vessel surface as a result of paddling the clay with a cord wrapped paddle.

A Cord marked sherd

        (2) smoothed-over-cordmarked: the potter has attempted to even out or smooth over the marks left by the cord wrapped paddle, thus some will be obliterated.

        (3) simple or check stamping: raised ridges and tiny check shapes left on the surface of a vessel as a result of paddling the clay with a carved wooden paddle.

B. Form: shape and declination of various vessel parts.

    1. Mouth: the vessel opening or orifice. The maximum diameter of the mouth can often be estimated by matching the curvature of an existing rim sherd with a circle of known diameter. The surviving rim section must be large enough to truly represent the vessel.

    2. Lip: the edge of the orifice where the inner and outer surfaces of the pot meet.

        a. shape: refers to the lip as seen in profile; determined by standing the rim with the lip pressed against a flat surface.

        (1) rounded: when the lip curves against a flat surface.

        (2) flat: when the lip lies flush against a flat surface.

        (3) beveled: where one edge of the lip lies flat and the other angles outward or inward.

        (4) narrowed and rounded: where there is only a very thin, curved edge to the lip.

        b. thickness: measured with a pair of calipers.

    3. Rim: on a vessel with a defined neck, this is usually the area between the lip and the point of maximum constriction. On a vessel lacking a defined neck, the rim is usually perceived as the lip and the area immediately adjacent to it; in this case the extent of the rim is indefinite.

        a. shape: refers to the rim section as seen in profile.

Ceramic Landmarks

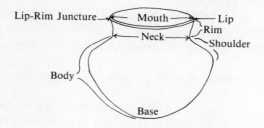

Basic Pottery Measurements

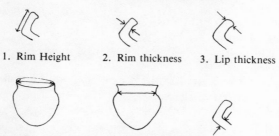

1. Rim Height   2. Rim thickness   3. Lip thickness

4. Diameter of mouth   5. Diameter of neck   6. Shoulder thickness

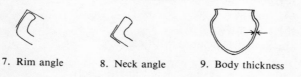

7. Rim angle   8. Neck angle   9. Body thickness

(1) straight: if you stand the rim vertically it forms a right angle with a flat surface.

(2) incurved: when stood vertically the rim curves inward.

(3) outcurved: when stood vertically the rim curves outward.

(4) S-shaped: the rim is wavy or appears as alternating curves in profile.

(5) collared or braced: the rim is reinforced or thickened with an extra piece of clay or doubled back upon itself so that it overhangs the neck of the pot.

b. height and thickness: measured with a pair of calipers. On a vessel with a defined neck, height is the distance between the lip and the shoulder. On a vessel where the extent of the rim is indefinite, height is indeterminate. Width is measured as the maximum thickness at the midpoint between the shoulder and the lip.

4. Neck: the narrowest part of the vessel, the area of maximum constriction.

5. Shoulder: the area between the neck and the point of maximum diameter.

   a. shape

    (1) flat: where the shoulder lies roughly horizontal to the

ground.

(2) curved: gently rounded.

(3) carinate: where the shoulder forms a sharp angle to the body of the vessel.

(4) vertical: where the shoulder lies roughly perpendicular to the ground.

    b. thickness: measured with calipers just below the angle of the neck.

6. Body: the main portion of the vessel including the area of maximum diameter. It is the portion of the pot to which the rim and base are attached. Sherds are normally identified as body sherds when they lack any sign of a lip.

    a. shape (as seen in profile)

        (1) globular

        (2) elliptical

        (3) elongated

    b. thickness: measured at the area of maximum thickness.

7. Base: the bottom of the vessel.

    a. shape

        (1) flat

        (2) rounded

        (3) conoidal: cone shaped

        (4) pointed

        (5) truncated

    b. thickness: measured with calipers.

C. Vessel form

1. jar: olla, vessel is constricted at the neck

2. bowl

3. bottle

4. pan

D. Paste: the material from which the vessel is made. It includes the plastic clay and the aplastic inclusions or temper.

1. Texture: this is an evaluation of the "surface feel," and appearance of the core as seen in cross-section of a sherd. Except to a few qualified specialists, this area of ceramic analysis is usually subjective.

    a. surface feel

        (1) fine

        (2) medium fine

        (3) medium coarse

        (4) coarse

    b. core

        (1) friable

        (2) crumbly

        (3) compact

        (4) porous

        (5) flaky

        (6) laminated

(7) contorted

2. Temper: general categories of temper can usually be detected from inspection of the cross-section of a sherd. More precise identification of tempering material including the size of individual particles and their mineral composition requires microscopic examination.

    a. kinds of temper

        (1) grit

            (a) crushed rock of some sort

            (b) sand

            (c) "gravel" (a term used by Henning, 1961, apparently referring to waterworn stone pebbles exceeding the size range of sand grains)

        (2) bone

        (3) shell

        (4) plant fiber or grass (seen as fibrous impressions in the clay since the original material is burned in firing).

        (5) grog (sherd fragments)

        (6) cell-temper (the result of leaching away of bone, shell, or limestone temper leaving the surface pitted).

    b. relative amount: usually described as abundant, moderate, or sparse.

    c. size: of the individual particles.

3. Color: the color of the exterior and interior surfaces, core, and any slip or paint. Color usually ranges from buff to black. Archaeologists use soil color charts such as the one by Munsell to describe pottery color. This results in the presence of a number/letter designation which stands for a particular hue, intensity, and chroma.

4. Hardness: this refers to the "scratchability" of the vessel surface. Archaeologists normally use mineral rocks as the standard for determining hardness. The Moh's scale of hardness ranges from #1 softest (talc, steatite) to #10 hardest (diamond).

E. Decoration: the decorative treatment (kind and method of application) found on a vessel. Most decorative motifs are described as curvilinear, rectilinear, zoomorphic, biomorphic and so on.

1. Incising: refers to the scratching, cutting or grooving of a line design onto the vessel surface. Usually the width and depth of the incised lines are given.

    a. trailing: is a form of incising executed by dragging across the vessel surface when the paste is still moist. The term "finger trailing" refers to trailed lines of a breadth and depth indicative of application with the forefinger.

    b. engraving: refers to the incising of a line design onto the vessel surface after firing. Engraved lines show a jagged edge where the fired clay has been chipped away. You find no residual clay along the edge of an engraved line as is commonly the case in incising where the wet clay is dispersed along the incised line.

2. Stamping: refers to impressing a texture or pattern onto the vessel surface by a number of different techniques.

Cord impression

Punctations are the predominate decoration on the Levsen Punctate ceramics of eastern Iowa.

a. cord impressed: single pieces of cord pressed into the paste.

b. fabric impressed: woven pieces of fabric pressed into the paste.

c. punctation: a blunt-ended object poked into the paste.

d. cord-wrapped stick stamp: stick wrapped with cordage pressed into the paste. If repeated this results in a discontinuous series of impressions.

e. simple stamped: grooved wooden paddle or thong wrapped paddle pressed or pounded onto the vessel surface.

f. dentate stamped: notched or toothed implement rolled across the vessel surface. This creates a continuous series of impressions.

g. rocker stamped: shell edge or other curved-edged object rocked back and forth over the vessel surface. This creates a continuous series of impressions.

h. bosses: bumps made by pushing the clay outward from the opposite surface.

3. Modeled additions: features, such as handles or effigy figures, built up by hand from the vessel surface, or modeled separately and added to the surface.

    a. strap handle: a handle wider than it is thick.

    b. loop handle: a handle nearly as thick as it is wide.

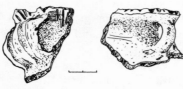

Strap handle   *Loop handle*

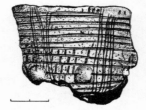

Incised lines and bosses are two decorative treatments found on Spring Hollow Incised pottery

    c. lugs: small, clay tabs.

    d. castellations: projections on the lip, or variations in the height of the rim.

    e. applique nodes: small lumps of clay added to the vessel surface.

    f. pinching: marks resulting from the fluting or squeezing of the clay usually along the edge of the lip.

    g. effigy forms: modeled animal or other figures added to the vessel.

    h. fillet: extra clay pieces or applique designs added onto the vessel surface.

4. Slip: a colored surface produced by the application of a liquid wash composed of colored clay and water. A slip is often difficult to distinguish from paint.

5. Paint: a colored surface produced by the application of a pigment composed of vegetable dye or certain minerals and water, before or after firing.

F. Ceramic items other than vessels.

    1. "pot lids": usually spherical clay disks.

    2. pipes

        a. elbow: a pipe with a right angle bend not unlike a modern pipe.

        b. tubular: a cigar-shaped pipe composed of a single piece (ie.) the bowl is not a separate feature distinct from the stem.

    3. Miscellaneous ceramic items of various shapes and with no obvious function have sometimes been interpreted as gaming pieces.

G. Classificatory terminology

    1. Ware: pottery sharing a number of attributes in common such as vessel form, paste, and temper. Ceramics within a ware are believed to be related in some way.

    2. Type: a subdivision of a ware. Ceramics which share a number of specific attributes in common, typically rim form and design, and are believed to be related in some way.

    3. Variety: a subdivision of a type. Closely related ceramics which show variation on a decorative theme, and are believed to represent styles within that type.

Early Woodland. Prehistoric Iowa ceramics, like projectile points, changed over time. The earliest pottery, found in Early Woodland times, is known primarily from sites in the eastern half of the state, and shows its strongest affinity to types in Illinois. These early ceramics include the following types: *Marion Thick, Black Sand Incised, Morton Incised,* and *Sisters Creek Punctate.*

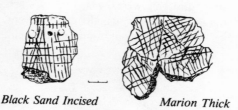

Black Sand Incised   *Marion Thick*

    These ceramics represent vessels with thick walls (.8 to 1.5 cm.), a coarse texture, soft paste, and heavy amounts of coarse, grit temper making the vessel seem almost overtempered. Surface color varies from yellow orange to dark brown or gray on the exterior and black on the interior. Early types, such as Marion Thick, were straight-sided forms with either a flat or round base, and interior cord marking. Otherwise, deep jar forms, with straight shoulders and conoidal bases predominate. Lips are flattened to rounded and sometimes rolled. The rim is straight. Most of these early types have a cord marked surface or one that was cord marked and then smoothed over. Decoration most commonly occurs on the rim and takes the form of incised lines or herringbone designs and punctates, arranged in vertical or horizontal rows. Fingernail punctates, pinching of the upper rim, and zones of punctates and bosses also occur. (A. Anderson, 1971; Griffin, 1952; Logan, 1976)

Middle Woodland — Havana Ware (Cedar Ware). The diagnostic pottery types of the Middle Woodland are those belonging to the Havana Ware category (defined on the basis of Illinois types) or certain analogous, indigenous Iowa types from the interior of eastern Iowa which have recently been labeled Cedar Ware (Benn and Thompson, 1977). Havana Ware includes *Neteler Stamped, Havana Cordmarked, Havana Zoned, Naples Stamped, Steuben Punctated,* and *Hummel Stamped.* Cedar Ware types are *Palo-Cordroughened, Palo Plain, Palo Stamped,* and *Palo Trailed.*

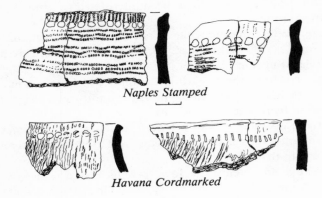

Naples Stamped

Havana Cordmarked

In general, the pottery in these ware groupings is composed of a coarse-textured, grainy, compact paste, with moderate amounts of angular crushed rock temper (usually granite). Outer surface colors are light grayish brown, buffs, and yellow browns; interiors are dark brown and black or gray. Vessel walls are thick, usually around 1 cm. Vessel forms are deep, elongated jars with nearly straight and vertical rims; flattened, bev-

Zones of decoration outlined by incising are a characteristic feature of Havana vessels.

eled, or rounded lips; slightly expanding shoulders; and conoidal or rounded bases. The exterior surface is cord marked, smoothed-over-cordmarked, or plain. Decoration is generally found around the rim and neck,
and characteristically is composed of zones of cord-wrapped stick impressions, dentate stamping, incising and tool notching. Punctations and
bosses are common. Applied zones of decoration are often outlined by
wide incised (trailed) lines. In contrast to their Havana Ware counterparts,
Cedar Ware types have their own decorative motifs and combinations of
decorations (although these are variations and recombinations of Illinois
Havana styles); and the ware itself appears to contain fewer types (see
Benn and Thompson, 1977: 21). (A. Anderson, 1971; Benn, 1976; Benn
and Thompson, 1977; Griffin, 1952; Logan, 1976; Straffin, 1971; Illinois
State Museum, 1952)

Middle Woodland Rowe Ware. Middle Woodland pottery from the
Glenwood locality of southwestern Iowa has been called Rowe Ware,
and has its closest Plains affiliation with Valley Cord Roughened Ware
of the Central Plains, and its closest Eastern Woodland affiliation with
Havana Tradition pottery of the Illinois River Valley. Rowe Ware has
been divided into two types on the basis of exterior surface treatment:
Rowe Cordmarked and *Rowe Plain.*

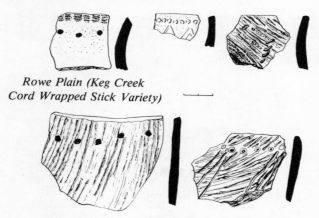

*Rowe Plain (Keg Creek
Cord Wrapped Stick Variety)*

Rowe Cordmarked (Pony Creek Punctate Variety)

Rowe Ware is comprised of elongated vessels with poorly defined,
smoothly curved shoulders and conoidal bases. Bases are substantially
thicker than rim, neck, or shoulder sherds. Rims range from straight to
gently flaring, a few are recurved or S-shaped. Lips are usually straight
and flattened, a few are beveled, a small percentage are rounded. The
paste is compact, the texture medium fine to medium coarse. Sherds are
grit-tempered. Color ranges from light brown and pink to very dark gray
on the exterior surface; interior color ranges from light brown to dark
gray. Firing clouds are common. Hardness ranges from 2 to 4.5. Exterior surfaces show vertical, diagonal, horizontal, or criss-cross cord-
marking. In some cases, the exterior surface has been smoothed over

after paddling. In rare instances surfaces are plain. Interior surfaces are poorly smoothed. Several sherds show incomplete smoothed-over-cordmarked surfaces. When present, decoration is confined mainly to the exterior surfaces of the rim. Decoration is usually in 3 vertical zones: cordwrapped stick, dentate stamp, or twisted cord impressions on the lip-rim exterior, below which is a horizontal band of punctates. Below the punctates on approximately ⅓ of the rims, some sort of trailed geometric design is present. This extends onto the shoulder area of the vessel. (Hill and Kivett, 1941; Kivett, 1952; Tiffany, 1978)

Transitional Period — Linn Ware. Ceramics transitional between Middle and Late Woodland pottery wares found in eastern Iowa sites are referred to as Linn Ware, and include *Spring Hollow Plain, Spring Hollow Incised, Spring Hollow Cord Impressed, Spring Hollow Brushed, Levsen Stamped, Levsen Punctated, Lane Farm Cord Impressed,* and *Lane Farm Stamped.*

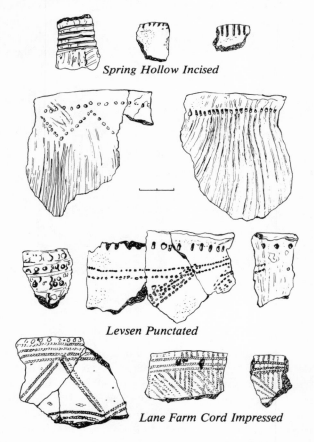

Spring Hollow Incised

Levsen Punctated

Lane Farm Cord Impressed

This pottery is fine textured; with moderate amounts of small grit, crushed rock and sand, temper; and generally thinner walls than previous wares. Exterior and interior surface colors range from buffs and browns to charcoal grays, with cores often darker or lighter than the vessel surface. Vessels tend to be more globular than earlier types, with bases rounded or conoidal. Rims are straight to slightly flaring (everted) with lips rounded, flattened, or sometimes everted. Vessels may expand at the shoulder more markedly than those of Havana Ware types. Vessel surfaces may be cord marked, smoothed-over-cord-marked, or plain. On some types decoration is confined to lip notching or cross hatching. On others, decoration takes the form of zoned patterns of fingernail and tool punctating, geometric incising, dentate and rocker stamping. Decoration can extend onto the shoulder of the vessel. Lane Farm types show a scraped and smoothed, or polished surface, and cord decoration probably produced by an impressed fabric sheet, which may anticipate the Late Woodland Fabric Impressed wares. (Benn, 1976; Logan, 1976; Benn and Thompson, 1977)

Late Woodland Madison Ware (Minnott's Ware). Northeast and east central Iowa types which appear after the 7th Century A.D. have been grouped into Madison Ware and Minnott's Ware categories. Types within each category include *Madison Plain, Madison Fabric Impressed, Minnott's Plain, Minnott's Fabric Impressed,* and *Hahn Fabric Impressed.*

The technique of fabric marking on pottery (Benn 1976)

The outstanding feature of this pottery is the presence of fabric impressions on the rim and neck of the vessel reflecting the use of a woven fabric collar which was applied to the soft clay as both a supporting and decorative form. Evidence suggests that wet clay was actually pressed against the interior of the woven collar. The wares are characterized by a fine, hard paste with a gritty surface texture, temper of finely crushed rock or sand, and very thin walls (2-6 mm. thick). Exterior is charcoal black to charcoal brown. Carbon smudges and firing clouds are occasionally present on the exterior surface and frequently on the interior surface. The interior surface is sometimes darker than the exterior and is usually charcoal black to brown. The core ranges in color from charcoal gray to brick red. Vessels are subglobular to globular in shape with rounded, conoidal, or round bases. Necks are straight and vertical, and rims may be straight or slightly flaring. On Minnott's Ware types, rims are straight or slightly flaring and can be castellated or squared with sharp junctures at the expanding shoulder. Lips are rounded, flattened,

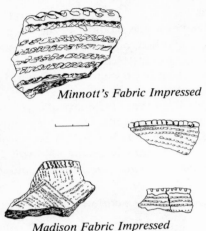

Minnott's Fabric Impressed

Madison Fabric Impressed

and notched, and on some Minnott's Ware, the lip is thickened. The bodies of these vessels are fabric marked and the rim and shoulders are usually imprinted with decorative woven fabric design. The design motifs produced by the woven fabric collar are highly variable. On Minnott's Fabric Impressed, the cords of the rim decoration tend not to be paired. (Baerreis, 1953; Beaubien, 1953; Keslin, 1957; Wittry, 1959; Logan, 1976; Benn, 1976)

Late Woodland — Sterns Creek Ware. Sterns Creek Ware includes two pottery types, *Sterns Creek Plain* and *Sterns Creek Tool Impressed* known from Late Woodland sites in the Missouri River area of southwestern Iowa and eastern Nebraska.

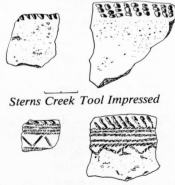

Sterns Creek Tool Impressed

Missouri Bluffs Cord Impressed

Sterns Creek vessels are small, vertically elongated jars with sub-conoidal bases, gently sloping shoulders, and slightly flaring rims with narrowed, rounded lips. The texture of the paste is medium fine to coarse, fairly compact, and brittle with some sherds tending to crumble. Temper is crushed granite. The color ranges from light buff to gray black and firing clouds are prevalent. Vessels show simple stamping on the exterior surface produced with a grooved or thong-wrapped paddle. The necks and rims are smoothed over and the bodies are partially smoothed over. The primary decorative treatment is a parallel band(s) of vertical or diagonal tool impressions around the exterior lip/rim juncture. In a few cases the tool impressions cut across the lip providing a scalloped effect. On some vessels the lip was left plain. (Strong, 1935; Wedel, 1940, 1959; 1961; Brown, 1967; Tiffany, 1977)

Late Woodland — Scalp Ware (Missouri Bluffs Cord Impressed Type). Scalp Ware includes pottery types found primarily in the Missouri River area of eastern South Dakota and adjacent parts of Nebraska and Iowa. The most prevalent type to date in Iowa is the Late Woodland *Missouri Bluffs Cord Impressed* which has its closest affinity to types of the Loseke Creek focus of Nebraska, particularly Feye Cord Impressed. It has been suggested that the cord impressed decoration on these ceramics is similar to that on fabric impressed wares further east such as Madison Fabric Impressed, and should be reexamined to see whether it resulted from the impression of a woven fabric sheet or collar.

Scalp Creek Ware, including Missouri Cord Impressed, includes globular vessels with outflaring rims, flattened or rounded lips, rounded shoulders, and rounded or conoidal bases. The paste is rough and angular with large, rounded grit (quartzite) temper. Surface color is light gray to buff with a dark gray to black core. Missouri Bluffs Cord Impressed has a smoothed-over-cordmarked exterior rim surface beneath the cord impressed decoration, and a cord marked body. The decorative treatment is a band of tool impressions or twisted cord impression on the exterior rim/lip juncture, below which is a series of single cord or twisted cord impressions forming a number of parallel, horizontal bands. A zig-zag or triangular shaped pendant of twisted cord or single cord impressions is usually placed below and joins the last horizontal band. On some vessels there is a zig-zag pendant through the horizontal band. Other Scalp Ware types are *Scalp Punctated, Scalp Cord Impressed, Ellis Plain, Ellis Cord Wrapped Rod, Ellis Cord Impressed,* and *Randall Incised.* (Keyes, 1949; Hurt, 1952; Kivett, 1952; Johnston, 1967; Tiffany, 1977)

Late Prehistoric — Nebraska Culture Wares at Glenwood. Four wares have been identified at the Late Prehistoric Nebraska Culture sites in the vicinity of Glenwood in southwestern Iowa. The four wares are distinguished almost exclusively on the basis of rim form. In general, all four wares were probably produced by modeling and paddling. The paste is medium fine to medium coarse with frequent to profuse amounts of grit, granite and sand, temper. The paste has a compact core and a crumbly or flaky texture. The exterior surface is gray to buff in color with firing clouds frequent. The core is orange to gray. Vessel surfaces were scraped and smoothed. Slip and paint occur rarely. Vessels are relatively thin, ranging from 3 to 16 mm. in thickness. Vessel shapes include medium to large jars, some small jars, bowls, and occasionally miniature vessels possibly the work of children. The lip on Nebraska Culture pottery is rounded, narrow rounded, occasionally flattened, beveled, or rolled. Plain, flaring or straight rims predominate although some types are braced, and some S-shaped. Jar forms have constricted necks which are incipient to absent in bowls. The shoulders are expanded to smoothly rounded. Occasionally shoulders are angular approaching a round, carinate form. Most vessel surfaces are cord marked or smoothed-over-cordmarked. Decoration includes finger pinching, punctations, or incising of the rim and/or lip, and incised and narrow trailed geometric lines on the shoulder area. Handles frequently occur, narrow, strap types being the most common. (Gunnerson, 1952; Ives, 1955; Anderson & Anderson, 1960; Anderson, 1961; Brown, 1967; Gradwohl, 1969)

McVey Ware Types

McVey Ware is characterized by simple, unthickened rims, straight to somewhat curving to flaring in form. Lips are usually rounded but may be flattened or thinned. McVey Ware types include *McVey Plain, McVey Rolled, McVey Tool Decorated, McVey Pinched* and *McVey Fillet*.

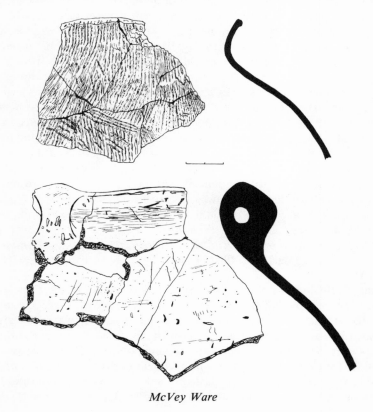

McVey Ware

Beckman Ware Types

Beckman Ware types have a braced rim: a rim thickened to a wedge-shape below the lip. At its juncture with the body, the rim narrows abruptly producing a collared effect. In cross-section this collared rim is wedge-shaped. The lip is usually rounded but may be sharp or flat. Lug handles are common. Beckman Ware types include *Beckman Pinched* or *Tool Impressed, Beckman Plain, Beckman Tool Decorated, Beckman Pinched Rim, Beckman Pinched Tooled.*

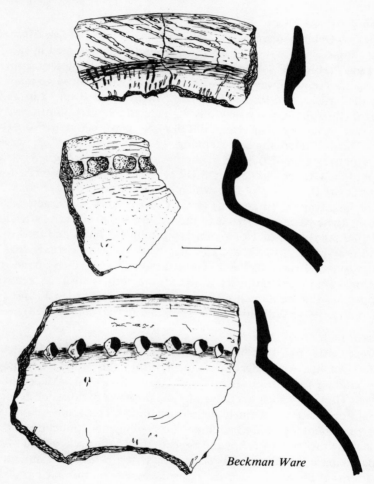

Beckman Ware

Swoboda Ware Types

Swoboda Ware also has collared rims but these are S-shaped in profile. The interior of the rim has a distinct concavity or channel above the neck. The lip is rounded to squared. It is also characterized by a rough, uneven surface which distinguishes it from the Foreman Ware category of Mill Creek ceramics. Swoboda types include *Swoboda Plain, Swoboda Cord Impressed, Swoboda Pinched* or *Tool Impressed, Swoboda Incised.*

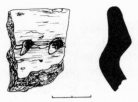

Swoboda Ware

Debilka Ware Types

The two Debilka Ware types, *Debilka Straight* and *Debilka Constricted,* are simple, shallow bowl forms with rounded or flattened lips.

Late Prehistoric — Great Oasis Pottery. Formerly pottery from Great Oasis sites in northwestern Iowa has been classified into two main wares on the basis of rim form: *Great Oasis Incised* and *Wedge Lip.* A third, *Great Oasis Plain,* was essentially an undecorated version of Great Oasis Incised. A more recent evaluation of Great Oasis ceramics from the upper Midwest (Henning and Henning, 1978) suggests the classification of this pottery into two ware groupings: *Great Oasis High Rim,* which would include the old Great Oasis Plain and Great Oasis Incised wares; and *Great Oasis Wedge Lip,* which corresponds to the previous Wedge Lip classification. In general, Great Oasis pottery is characterized by a fairly dense paste with sparse to moderate amounts of grit (often granite or fine sand) temper. Color ranges from lighter buffs and tans to grays and gray-black. Vessels are globular in shape with a constricted neck, high rounded shoulder, and rounded base. The surface of the rim interior is smoothed and often polished, the body is cord marked with its upper portion smoothed over and frequently polished. (Wilford, 1945; Henning, 1971; Williams, 1975; Henning and Henning, 1978)

Great Oasis High Rim

Great Oasis High Rim has straight rims (parallel-sided in profile) and a flattened lip. An undecorated form within this ware (seemingly corresponding to the old Great Oasis Plain) does exist. Decorated Great Oasis High Rim is characterized by the presence of zones of decoration: tool impressions and finely incised decorative motifs on the lip, with a narrow band of incised oblique lines, elongated punctates or cross-hatching just below the lip; and beneath this to the neck, a field of closely spaced parallel, horizontal incised lines over which are superimposed patterns of oblique incisions, zig-zag meanders, or multiple parallel lines, pendant triangles, hatched triangles, and biomorphic designs.

Great Oasis Wedge Lip

Great Oasis Wedge Lip is characterized by a generally low and outcurving rim, wedge-shaped in profile. The lip surface is flattened and generally oriented at an oblique angle. Some sherds appear to have a thickened rim. Decoration is confined to the flattened lip surface or the lip-rim exterior margin and takes the form of cross-hatching, tool impressions, or a combination of these. A plain, undecorated form also occurs, implying two types within this ware category.

Great Oasis Plain Wedge Lip

Great Oasis Decorated Wedge Lip

Great Oasis High Rim (Great Oasis Incised)

Late Prehistoric — Mill Creek Pottery. Four wares have been identified at the Late Prehistoric Mill Creek sites along the Big and Little Sioux Rivers and their tributaries in northwestern Iowa. Three of the wares are distinguishable on the basis of rim form. The fourth, Mill Creek Ware, includes a variety of forms which are believed to show a strong affinity to pottery from Middle Mississippian tradition sites such as the prehistoric city of Cahokia. In general, all of the Mill Creek wares share a well consolidated paste which ranges from coarse with excessive amounts of grit temper (crushed granite, granite and sand, crushed limestone, limestone and sand), to fine with sparse amounts of temper. The interior surface color of Mill Creek vessels is gray or buff, the exterior often a shade of buff with firing clouds visible. Except for the various Mill Creek Ware vessel forms, vessels in the other three ware categories are generally sub-globular in shape with rounded bases. Surfaces are plain or smoothed-over-cord marked. A red slip and a black paint occur especially on vessels within the Mill Creek Ware. Types within each ware are determined on the basis of rim design and rim design application. (Hurt, 1951; Lehmer, 1951, 1954; Hurt, 1954; Fugle, 1962; Ives, 1962; Henning, 1969; Anderson, 1972)

Sanford Ware

Subglobular vessels with short, thickened rims and constricted necks characterize Sanford Ware. Rims are strongly flared to nearly vertical and rarely over 3 cm. in height. Lips are usually flat or beveled to the exterior. The rim is usually thickest at the lip. Component types are *Mitchell Modified Lip, Kimball Modified Lip,* and *Sanford Plain.*

Chamberlain Ware

The Chamberlain Ware category includes subglobular vessels with high, straight, slightly to strongly flaring rims and constricted necks. The vessel lip is normally rounded or flattened. Types include *Chamberlain Incised, Chamberlain Incised Triangle, Chamberlain Cross-hatched.*

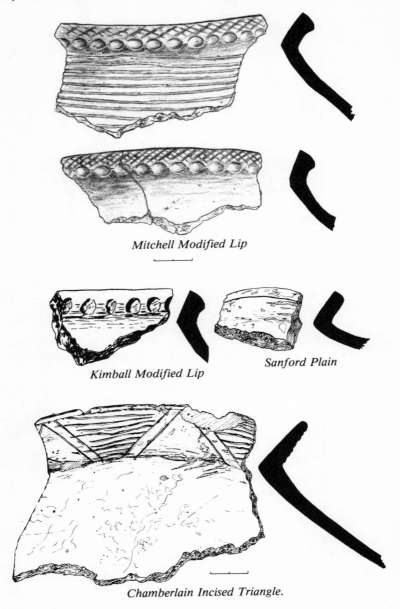

Mitchell Modified Lip

Kimball Modified Lip   *Sanford Plain*

Chamberlain Incised Triangle.

Foreman Ware
Foreman Ware is composed of subglobular vessels with S-shaped rim profiles ranging from broad, gently curving profiles to very angular almost Z-shaped profiles. Lips are flattened, sometimes rounded, seldom thicker than the rim walls. Component types are *Foreman Plain, Fore-*

man Cord Impressed, Foreman Cord Impressed Triangle, Foreman Incised, Foreman Incised Triangle, Foreman Cross-hatched.

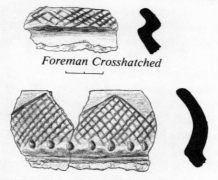

Foreman Crosshatched

Foreman Crosshatched Triangle

Mill Creek Ware

Traditionally Mill Creek Ware has been a catch-all category of different vessel forms including bowls, pans, seed jars, bottles, and miniature vessels, which were believed to be directly related to ceramics in the Middle Mississippian Tradition. Types include *Mill Creek bowls and pans, Mill Creek seed jars, Mill Creek Vertical Neck, Mill Creek Red Film.*

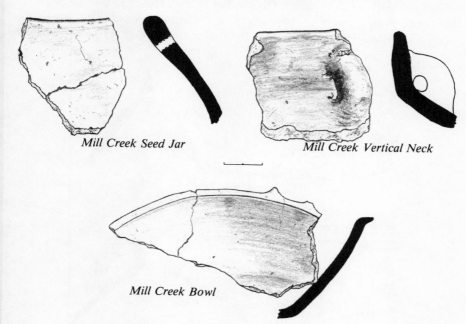

Mill Creek Seed Jar

Mill Creek Vertical Neck

Mill Creek Bowl

Late Prehistoric — Oneota Pottery. Ceramics associated with the Late Prehistoric Oneota manifestation in Iowa are noted for their variability and difficulty in typing. The diagnostic feature of Oneota pottery is the presence of shell tempering. Grit tempered ceramics occur as a minor ware, *Correctionville Grit Tempered,* at sites in the Little Sioux Valley area, and seem to increase in frequency at Oneota sites in South Dakota. The two primary shell tempered categories defined to date are *Correctionville Shell-tempered Ware* with its *Correctionville Trailed,* the diagnostic type of Iowa's equivalent of the Blue Earth Focus; and *Allamakee Trailed,* the diagnostic type of the Orr Focus. In general, Oneota ceramics are buff to buff gray in color with a bluish gray core, a smooth surface, and shell temper comprising 20% of the paste. Cell tempering, where the shell has been leached leaving a pitted surface, is particularly common in the eastern Iowa sites where soils are generally more acidic. Vessels are characteristically elliptical to globular shaped jars, with rounded shoulders and broadly rounded bases. A straight rim usually flares outward from a constricted neck. Lips are frequently modified with decoration. Where plain lips are found they may be narrowed and thinned. Vessel walls range from 2 to 11 mm. in thickness. Vessels include miniature jars as well as large forms up to 40 cm. in diameter. The exterior surface of most vessels has been wiped and smoothed. Decoration was applied to the lip, rim, and shoulder area of the pot. The lip has frequently been notched giving a rippled effect to the rim. Shoulder decoration includes trailed line motifs frequently based on variations of grouped diagonal and straight lines, often in chevrons, supplemented with punctates. Design motifs are repeated around the vessel extending from the neck on downward. Decoration rarely extends below the point of maximum diameter. Slipping and painting occasionally occur. (Wedel, M.M., 1959; Wedel, W., 1959; Henning, 1961; Harvey, 1979)

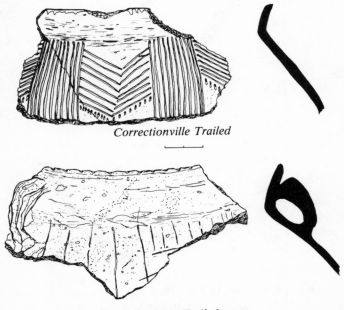

Correctionville Trailed

Allamakee Trailed

100

Correctionville Shell-tempered Ware
Correctionville Trailed Type

Prehistoric Oneota pottery found in the Little Sioux Valley area has been named Correctionville Trailed. It is represented by elliptical to round jar forms with broad, smoothly curved shoulders and an orifice roughly half the diameter of the shoulder. Small bowls also occur. The height of most vessels is ¾ to the same as the diameter. The rim height ranges from 15 to 40 mm. Nodes, tabs, effigies and two opposing, small strap handles frequently occur. Surfaces are smoothed and occasionally polished. Lips are usually narrowed and decorated with notching. Rim decoration takes the form of tool impressions from the lip to the rim interior, trailing on the rim interior, and occasionally tool impressions on the rim exterior. Shoulders are generally decorated with trailed line motifs: opposed diagonals, vertical lines, and chevrons. Occasionally shoulders are left plain. Tool impressions, short trailed lines, punctates, and (rarely) crosses may embellish shoulder motifs. Trailed lines are 1-8 mm. wide; finger trailing from 11-14 mm. Motifs are made up of closely spaced lines and rarely extend over more than ¼ of the shoulder surface. Small strap handles are sometimes decorated with vertical lines, punctates, and tool impressions.

Correctionville Grit Tempered Ware

This is a minority ware at sites in the Little Sioux Valley. The outstanding characteristic of this ware is its fine gravel temper (Henning, 1961). Otherwise it is generally similar in other attributes to Correctionville Trailed.

Allamakee Trailed Type

Allamakee Trailed represents the late prehistoric and proto-historic Oneota pottery found in the Upper Iowa River Valley area. It is also represented by elliptical to round jars and occasionally by small bowls. Vessels have a smoothly curved to steeply sloping shoulder. The rim is slightly outcurved to outsloping, ranging from vertical to flaring. Rims are generally higher than on Correctionville Trailed types, ranging from 17 to 70 mm.; and thin towards the lip. The lip is usually decorated, but where plain, is rounded. Frequently two strap handles or occasionally loop handles are present. Nodes and tab handles are rare. Lip decoration takes the form of notching and finger punctating. The rim is decorated by tool impression. Shoulder decoration is composed of motifs executed by trailing, punctating, or a combination of the two. Motifs include vertical lines, triangles, and oblique lines. Trailed lines are 1-2 mm. wide, finger trailing from 12-14 mm. Strap handles are decorated with grooves, vertical trailed lines, and punctates. Triangular to tapering strap handles are decorated with bisected "v" motifs. Loop handles are notched or plain.

REFERENCES

Alex, Robert A.
n.d. Unpublished PhD. dissertation, University of Wisconsin-Madison.
In progress.

Anderson, Adrian and Barbara Anderson
1960 Pottery Types of the Glenwood Focus. **Journal of the Iowa Archeological Society**, Vol. 9 (4): 12-39.

Anderson, Adrian
1951 The Glenwood Sequence: A Local Sequence for a Series of Archeological Manifestations in Mills County, Iowa. **Journal of the Iowa Archeological Society**, Vol. 10 (3).
1971 Review of Iowa River Valley Archaeology, in Prehistoric Investigations, Marshall McKusick (ed). **Office of the State Archaeologist, Report #3.** Iowa City.

Anderson, Duane
1972 The Ceramic Complex at the Brewster Site (13CK15): A Mill Creek Component in Northwestern Iowa. Doctoral dissertation, **University Microfilms,** University of Michigan, Ann Arbor.

Baerreis, David A.
1953 Blackhawk Village Site (Da5) Dane County, Wisc. **Journal of the Iowa Archeological Society**, Vol. 2: 5-20.

Beaubien, Paul L.
1953 Cultural Variation within Two Woodland Mound Groups of Northeast Iowa. **American Antiquity,** Vol. 19 (1): 56-66.

Benn, David
1976 The Woodland Cultures of Northeast Iowa (A.D. 300-800): A Perspective from Hadfields Cave Site. Doctoral dissertation, **University Microfilms,** University of Michigan, Ann Arbor.

Benn, David and Dean Thompson
1977 The Young Site, Linn County, Iowa and Comments on Woodland Ceramics. **Journal of the Iowa Archeological Society,** Vol. 24: 1-61.

Brown, Lionel
1967 Pony Creek Archaeology. **Publications in Salvage Archaeology 5. Smithsonian Institution River Basin Surveys.**

Caldwell, Warren W.
1961 Archaeological Investigations at the Coralville Reservoir, Iowa. **Bureau of American Ethnology, Bulletin 179, River Basin Survey Papers, 22:** 79-148.

Fugle, Eugene
1962 Mill Creek Culture and Technology. **Journal of the Iowa Archeological Society,** Vol. 2 (4): 76-81.

Gradwohl, David M.
1969   Prehistoric Villages in Eastern Nebraska. **Nebraska State Histori-cal Society Publications, 4.** Lincoln.

Griffin, James
1952   Some Early and Middle Woodland Pottery Types in Illinois, in Hopewellian Communities in Illinois. Thorne Deuel (ed). **Illinois State Museum Scientific Papers** #5. Springfield.

Gunnerson, James H.
1952   Some Nebraska Culture Pottery Types. **Plains Archaeological Conference Newsletter,** Vol. 5 (3): 39-49.

Harvey, Amy E.
1979   Oneota Culture in Northwestern Iowa. **Office of the State Ar-chaeologist, Report 12,** Iowa City.

Henning, Dale
1961   Oneota Ceramics in Iowa. **Journal of the Iowa Archeological Society,** Vol. 11 (2).
1969   Ceramics from the Mill Creek Sites, in Climatic Change and the Mill Creek Culture of Iowa, Pt. 2., Dale Henning (ed), **Journal of the Iowa Archeological Society,** Vol. 15.
1971   Great Oasis Culture Distributions, in Prehistoric Investigations, Marshall McKusick (ed). **Office of the State Archaeologist, Report 3.** Iowa City.

Henning, Dale R. and Elizabeth Henning
1978   Great Oasis Ceramics, in Some Studies of Minnesota Prehistoric Ceramics: Papers Presented at the First Council for Minnesota Archeology Symposium — 1976, Alan R. Woolworth and Mark A. Hall (ed). **Occasional Publications in Minnesota Anthro-pology, No. 2.** Ft. Snelling, St. Paul.

Hill, A. T. and Marvin Kivett
1941   Woodlandlike Manifestations in Nebraska. **Nebraska History Mazagine,** Vol. 21 (3): 145-242.

Hurt, Wesley
1951   Report of the Investigation of the Swanson Site, 39BR16, Brule County, South Dakota. **South Dakota Archaeological Commis-sion, Archaeological Studies Circular #3.**
1952   Report on the Investigations of the Scalp Creek Site, 39GR1, and the Ellis Creek Site, 39Gr2, Gregory County, South Dakota. **Ar-chaeological Studies Circular, #4.** South Dakota Archaeological Commission.
1954   Pottery Types of the Over Focus, South Dakota in **Prehistoric Pottery of the Eastern United States.** Museum of Anthropology, University of Michigan, Ann Arbor.

Illinois State Museum
1952   Hopewellian Communities in Illinois. **Illinois Scientific Papers,**
       Vol. 5. Springfield.

Ives, John
1955   Glenwood Ceramics. **Journal of the Iowa Archeological Society,**
       Vol. 4 (3 & 4).
1962   Mill Creek Pottery, **Journal of the Iowa Archeological Society,**
       Vol. 11 (3): 1-57.

Johnston, Richard B.
1967   The Hitchell Site. **Publications in Salvage Archaeology, 3.**
       Smithsonian Institution River Basin Surveys.

Keslin, Richard O.
1957   A Preliminary Report on the Hahn (Dg 1 and Dg 2) and Horicon
       (Dg5) Sites, Dodge County, Wisconsin. **Wisconsin Archeologist,**
       Vol. 39 (4): 191-273.

Keyes, Charles
1949   Four Iowa Archeologies with Plains Affiliations. **Proceedings of
       the 5th Plains Conference for Archeology, No. 1.** Lab. of An-
       thropology, University of Nebraska: 96-97. Lincoln.

Kivett, Marvin F.
1952   Woodland Sites in Nebraska. **Nebraska State Historical Society
       Publications in Anthropology, #1.**

Lehmer, Donald J.
1951   Pottery Types from the Dodd Site, Oahe Reservoir, South
       Dakota. **Plains Archaeological Conference Newsletter,** Vol. 4 (2).
1954   Archaeological Investigations in the Oahe Dam Area, South
       Dakota, 1950-1951. **Bureau of American Ethnology Bulletin 158,
       River Basin Survey Papers #7.**

Logan, Wilfred D.
1976   Woodland Complexes in Northeastern Iowa. **U.S. Dept of the In-
       terior National Park Service Publications in Archaeology, 15.**

Riegger, Hal
1972   **Primitive Pottery.** New York: Van Nostrand Reinhold Co.

Shepard, Anna O.
1965   Ceramics for the Archaeologist. **Carnegie Institute of Washing-
       ton, Publication 609.**

Straffin, Dean
1971   Wolfe Havana Hopewell Site, in Prehistoric Investigations, Mar-
       shall McKusick (ed) . **Office of the State Archaeologist Report 3.**
       Iowa City.

Strong, William Duncan
1935 An Introduction to Nebraska Archaeology. **Smithsonian Institution Miscellaneous Collections 93.**

Tiffany, Joseph
1977 Artifacts from the Sharps Site: A Sterns Creek Component in Southwest Iowa. **Journal of the Iowa Archeological Society,** Vol. 24: 84-124.
1978 A Model for Changing Settlement Patterns for the Mill Creek Culture of Northwest Iowa: An Analysis from Chan-ya-ta Site (13BV1), Buena Vista County, Iowa. Doctoral dissertation, **University Microfilms,** University of Michigan, Ann Arbor.
1978 Middle Woodland Pottery Typology from Southwest Iowa. **Plains Anthropologist** 23 (81): 169-182.

Wedel, Mildred Mott
1959 Oneota Sites on the Upper Iowa River. **Missouri Archaeologist,** Vol. 21 (2-4).

Wedel, Waldo
1940 Cultural Sequence in the Central Great Plains. **Smithsonian Institution Miscellaneous Collections 100:** 291-352.
1959 An Introduction to Kansas Archaeology. **Bureau of American Ethnology Bulletin 174.**
1961 **Prehistoric Man on the Great Plains.** Norman: University of Oklahoma Press.

Wheeler, Richard
1952 Plains Ceramic Analysis: A Checklist of Features and Descriptive Terms. **Plains Archaeological Conference Newsletter, #5:** 29-36.

Whiteford, Andrew Hunter
1970 **North American Indian Arts.** New York: Golden Press.

Wilford, Lloyd
1945 Three Villages of the Mississippian Pattern in Minnesota. **American Antiquity,** Vol. 11 (1): 35-40.

Williams, Patricia McAlister
1975 The Williams Site (13PM50): A Great Oasis Component in Northwest Iowa. **Journal of the Iowa Archeological Society,** Vol. 22: 1-34.

Wittry, Warren
1959 Archeological Studies of Four Wisconsin Rock Shelters. **Wisconsin Archeologist,** Vol. 40 (4).

Chapter 8

Bone Artifacts

In North America the presence of abundant large game animals allowed Native peoples in three major culture areas — the Arctic, Subarctic, and Plains — to excell in the production and utilization of bone artifacts. Bone implements related to skin and hideworking occur throughout the prehistoric sequence in Iowa, however, it is in the Late Prehistoric Mill Creek sites of the northwestern part of the state that we find a florescence in bone technology. By A.D. 1000, the semi-sedentary Mill Creek hunter-farmers had mastered the art of translating byproducts of the hunt into functional and decorative artifacts. Doubtlessly, their proximity to the large bison herds of the Plains fostered this development.

Bone is a material which survives best in a dry climate and in alkaline soils. If exposed to the elements or incorporated in a wet, acid deposit, it is rarely preserved. For these reasons, bone artifacts are archaeologically less well represented than those of stone or pottery. At some sites, bone remains are nonexistent, and rarely is bone preserved as a surface find. Thus, bone preservation in the earlier Iowa sites, at sites in more humid areas of the state, and at those in regions having acidic soils, has probably not been as good as at later sites, and at those in drier, more alkaline contexts. Nevertheless, keeping these conditions of preservation in mind, there is no doubt that in Iowa, the Mill Creek Culture excelled over others in the utilization of bone and in the production of a wide variety of bone artifacts.

In general, bone artifacts have had limited value as diagnostic markers of prehistoric cultures or time periods. All Native Iowa peoples throughout prehistory were, at least in part, hunters. Certain bone hideworking implements span thousands of years of time with no discernible changes in style. Because bone tools took their shape, in part, from the faunal elements from which they were derived, they are fairly uniform in appearance from site to site and over time. Like projectile points, they were produced by reductive techniques, and their form was determined largely by technical and functional requirements. Unlike projectile points, they have not been used as relative temporal indicators. This is partially related to their uniformity over time, and also to their differential preservation from site to site. Whereas stone points are virtually indestructable, this is not the case with bone.

Certainly the occurrence of bone implements at a site reflects cultural preferences, particularly those related to the procurement of game animals. The Mill Creek people at the Phipps Site near Chrerokee, for instance, appear to have altered their preferences in game animals over time. The early levels at the site contain a higher percentage of deer. At about A.D. 1200 bison begin to become predominate at the site. This may be a reflection of changing environmental conditions in the area as

106

well as cultural preference. The appearance of some bone artifacts also correlates in time with major economic changes and innovations. Bone gardening tools such as the scapula hoe are a clue to the adoption of horticulture in the prehistoric economy. And some bone tool types or the methods for their production do seem culture specific. The characteristic bulbous-ended fish hook found at Mill Creek sites appears limited in its distribution to the related cultures of the Middle Missouri Tradition of western Iowa and eastern South Dakota.

Any discussion of bone technology demonstrates the interrelationship of economic activities in a prehistoric society. In order to acquire the raw materials and produce finished artifacts a complex body of knowledge and skill was required to locate, stalk, kill, and dismember game animals; and to cut, split, grind, steam, bend, polish and haft the chosen element to convert it into a functional implement. Stone artifacts directly associated with bone tool technology include spears, darts and arrowheads, knives, scrapers, serrated blades, chisels, gravers, abraders and drills.

Bone artifacts in Iowa

In the following section we have described those bone artifacts most commonly found in Iowa sites. Since most researchers discuss these in reference to the particular faunal element from which they were derived, the accompanying illustration is provided in order to demonstrate the source of faunal elements used in bone tool technology.

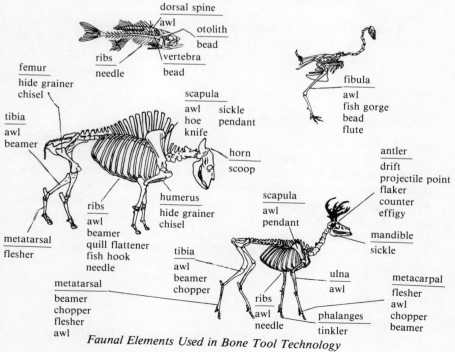

Faunal Elements Used in Bone Tool Technology

Skin and hideworking tools

Awls: the following elements were modified into sharply pointed tools used to pierce skins and hides prior to sewing, and in mat and basket making:
1. splintered rib, scapula, and tibia of bison or deer
2. quartered section of a deer metatarsal or metacarpal
3. deer ulna
4. bird fibula
5. dorsal spine of fish

Needles and/or pins: thin strips of bone from animal ribs or other elements were manufactured into implements used in sewing or matting. Some so-called needles may have been hair ornaments or portions of bracelets.

Fleshers: the distal end of a bison metatarsal and deer canon bone was serrated or beveled to form a tool used in scraping hides and removing fat and flesh.

Beamers: deer or elk tibia, deer metatarsals, and bison ribs were beveled at their ends to produce a tool used to remove hair from hides.

Hide grainers: the proximal end of bison humeri and possibly the proximal end of the femur were cut to expose the cancellous interior surface of the bone. This surface was used as an abrasive to smooth and reduce hides to a uniform thickness.

Drifts: a cylindrical section was cut from the shaft of a deer antler and rounded or squared, and smoothed to produce a multi-purpose tool whose function included rubbing and grinding skins, and flattening porcupine quills.

"Quill flattener": flat, spatulate object usually manufactured from a section of bison rib. These were probably multipurpose tools useful in flattening porcupine quills, smoothing and scraping the surface of a pot before firing, and flattening rushes and grasses used in weaving and basketry.

Hunting and fishing implements

Antler projectile points: projectile points were manufactured from the conical tips of deer antlers. These may have served as real projectiles, and may also have been used as the tips for willow javelins in the "snowsnake game", as they were historically.

Fish hooks: hooks manufactured from pieces of mammal bone, including bison ribs, were used in line fishing and possibly as grappling hooks. Mill Creek fish hooks are characterized by a bulbous shaft end.

Fish gorges: splinters of bird bone sharpened at both ends and used in line fishing.

Horticultural implements

Hoes: hoes used in gardening by Late Prehistoric peoples were manufactured from bison scapulas. Scapula hoes vary in the degree to which the

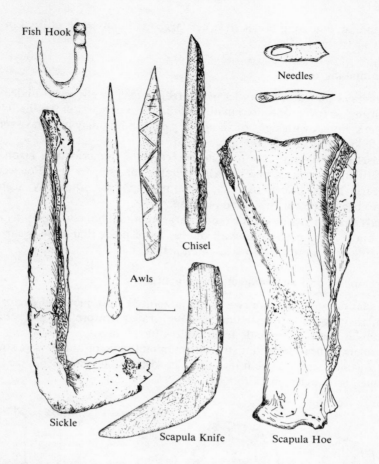

Fish Hook

Needles

Chisel

Awls

Sickle

Scapula Knife

Scapula Hoe

original bone was modified to permit attachment to a handle. On the simple type (like those found in Mill Creek sites) the head of the scapula bearing the glenoid cavity was retained without modification. In the notched variety (used by some Nebraska Culture people) a notch was placed in the costal margin of the glenoid cavity. Scapula hoes are particularly common at Mill Creek sites.

Knives: the flat section of a bison scapula was worked into a straight-edged, blunt-ended knife. Based on ethnographic analogy, these are believed to have been particularly useful in the cutting and scraping of squash, and are commonly referred to as squash knives.

Sickles: a bison scapula was split longitudinally and its spine was thinned to form a sickle. A deer mandible was also used as a sickle. On some mandibles the lower edge has been cut away attesting to their modification, but on others, the only clue to their use is in the presence of polish.

Hoe or scoop: a bison horn core with the attached portion of the frontal bone still attached was used as a digging tool or as a scoop. These are a common item in Mill Creek sites.

Chopping tool: a deer metatarsal or metacarpal was longitudinally halved and the proximal end reworked to form a gouge-like blade for chopping. The long bones of other large mammals were utilized in this way as well.

Toolmaking tools

Flakers or punches: the antler prong from a deer or elk was rounded and polished to form tools used in direct or indirect percussion flaking. Other bone splinters with signs of smoothing or grinding may also have served as flaking implements.

Chisel or wedge: a section from the femur or humerus of a bison was modified to create a beveled edge suitable for use as a chisel or wedge. Wedge-shaped beaver incisors, sometimes split longitudinally, seem to have been used for this same purpose.

Shaft straightener or shaft wrench: large mammal bones (frequently ribs) or antler were perforated with one or more holes that show wear suggesting they were used to straighten arrow shafts.

Ornaments and miscellaneous bone artifacts

Beads: ornamental jewelry was manufactured from pieces of perforated antler or bone, fish vertebrae, and perforated fish otoliths (ear stones). Tubular beads were made from hollow bird bones.

Armlets or bracelets: thin strips of mammal bone or antler were soaked or steamed and then bent into bracelet form. Some may also have functioned as bangles on clothing.

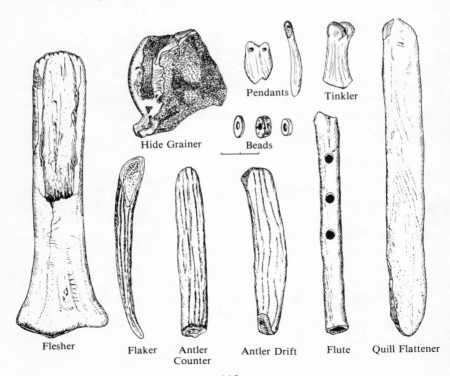

Pendants   Tinkler

Hide Grainer   Beads

Flesher   Flaker   Antler Counter   Antler Drift   Flute   Quill Flattener

Pendants: pieces of mammal bone or turtle carapace were cut into shapes and polished for pendants.

Tinklers: perforated deer phalanges probably hung on clothing. Both drilled and notched varieties occur. They are particularly common and diverse in Mill Creek sites.

Counters: short, square-ended segments of deer or elk antler were used as game counters or tally sticks.

Antler effigies: the tine from a deer or elk antler was cut into various effigy shapes; function unknown.

Bone flutes: the hollow long bone from birds were perforated with holes on one side and used as flutes. The oldest such artifact in Iowa occured in Horizon I at the Cherokee Sewer Site.

Turtle shell bowls: the carapace of a turtle functioned as a vessel. This artifact is common in Middle Woodland sites.

Turtle shell rattles: The carapace of a turtle was filled with pebbles, frequently of white quartz, and used as a shaker or rattle.

REFERENCES

Baerreis, David A.
1968   Artifact Descriptions: Bone, Stone and Shell, in Climatic Change and the Mill Creek Culture of Iowa, Part 1, Dale Henning (ed). **Journal of the Iowa Archeological Society,** Vol. 15.

Fugle, Eugene
1962   Mill Creek Culture and Technology. **Journal of the Iowa Archeological Society,** Vol. 11 (4).

Lehmer, Donald J.
1971   Introduction to Middle Missouri Archeology. **Anthropological Papers 1,** National Park Service, U.S. Department of the Interior.

Olsen, Stanley
1960   Post-Cranial Skeletal Characters of **Bison** and **Bos. Papers of the Peabody Museum of Archaeology and Ethnology,** Vol. 35 (4). Cambridge: Harvard University.
1968   Fish, Amphibian and Reptile Remains from Archaeological Sites, Part 1: Southeastern and Southwestern United States. **Papers of the Peabody Museum of Archaeology and Ethnology,** Vol. 56 (2). Cambridge: Harvard University.

Whiteford, Andrew Hunter
1970   **North American Indian Arts.** New York: Golden Press.

Chapter 9

Paleo-Indian Period

The earliest period in Iowa prehistory is sometimes referred to as the "Paleo-Indian" or "Big-Game Hunting" stage. It represents the first time that we find evidence of people living in the state. The remains of even earlier people have been found in North, Central and South America and suggest that the Western Hemisphere was colonized by 20,000 years ago and possibly earlier. It is believed that the very earliest immigrants entered the New World from Asia at various times throughout the last "Ice Age," or Pleistocene, when vast ice sheets partially covered the northern parts of North America and Eurasia. These ice sheets, or glaciers, locked up thousands of cubic miles of water, thereby lowering sea levels on a world-wide scale and exposing many areas of land formerly covered by water. One of these was an area beneath what is now the Bering Straits, a narrow strip of water which separates northeastern Siberia and western Alaska. It is believed that at several times during the Pleistocene when sea levels were lowered, this area emerged as dry land forming a broad bridge between the two continents. Across this bridge (sometimes referred to as Beringia) both plant and animal species gradually migrated, including the first human immigrants. Since the interior of Alaska appears to have been ice-free at these times, there was an open corridor south into North America. Some scientists believe, however, that this area would have been swampy and difficult to traverse. With sea levels lowered as much as 600 feet, the new immigrants could have come down the Northwest Coast. If so, that evidence is now under water.

"Beringia", the Bering Straits Land Bridge, is indicated by the hatched area.

The earliest Americans were probably seasoned hunters, who crossed over Beringia in search of caribou, musk ox, and at one time, the mammoth. Over generations, their descendants slowly drifted southward. In Canada, they would have encountered North America's two major ice sheets, the Cordilleran to the west, and the Laurentide to the east. Geological evidence suggests an ice-free corridor between these two which would have allowed passage southward. Such a corridor was probably wet and marshy and may have been more easily traversed during

112

periods of cold.

So far, Iowa has not revealed the remains of these very early inhabitants. Evidence of their descendants, the people of the Paleo-Indian period, is itself somewhat limited and has come almost exclusively from finds of lanceolate projectile points discovered on the surface of the ground. While the maximum time range for the Paleo-Indian period in

The Imperial Mammoth of North America was hunted by Paleo-Indian people

A Clovis spearpoint hafted to its shaft

North America may extend from 15,000 to 6,000 B.P. (Before Present), the earliest remains in Iowa are perhaps 12,000 years old. They consist of Clovis spearpoints of the so-called "Llano Culture."

At sites outside of Iowa, Clovis points have been found together with the remains of large extinct game animals such as the mammoth, horse, camel, and certain forms of bison which Clovis people hunted. The name "Big-Game Hunting" stage refers to the importance that these animals seemed to have had in the economy of these early Americans. So far in Iowa, Clovis points have been found only from the surface of the ground or in disturbed contexts. In 1965, on the east side of Hare Run, a small tributary of the Cedar River in Cedar County, a cache of some 11 complete and fragmentary points was recovered from the Rummels-Maske Site. These specimens were in the plowzone and had been disturbed as a result of farming.

The next Paleo-Indian "culture" represented in Iowa is the "Folsom Culture." The Folsom culture as it is known elsewhere in North America is typically represented at kill sites where a second variety of extinct bison was hunted. Here Folsom spearpoints are the most typical artifact found associated with these animal remains. Once again, Iowa has produced only surface finds of Folsom points.

The remains of later Paleo-Indian peoples are also present in Iowa, including the only example of a Paleo-Indian find from an excavated site. Artifacts of these later peoples elsewhere in North America have been grouped into what is referred to as the "Plano Culture." It is characterized by a number of lanceolate projectile points which generally lack fluting. Some of these points show a pattern of long, thin, pressure-flaked scars which run horizontally across their surface. Among the many types are Meserve, Milnesand, Browns Valley, Portales, Angostura, Eden, Agate Basin, Hanna, Duncan, Midland, Hell Gap, Cascade, Plainview, Scottsbluff, and Dalton. Once again, many of the artifacts of the Plano culture are found associated with game animals killed by Plano hunters. In some instances, these are modern species of bison, antelope and others. In Iowa, a number of Plano point types have been found as surface finds at various locations. Excavations in the lower level (Horizon III) at the Cherokee Sewer Site produced the remains of a possible Agate Basin point in association with modern bison in a context which dates to ca. 8600 years ago. A portion of a possible Scottsbluff type point was recovered from the excavation of the Soldow Site in Webster County.

By the Late Paleo-Indian period, hunters were no longer killing mammoth. With the retreat of the glaciers and the gradual return to warmer conditions, many Pleistocene species became extinct. Environmental changes, predation by hunters, disease, or a combination of all three, have been suggested as possible causes. With the disappearance of the mammoth, dire wolf, saber-toothed cat, ground sloth, and camel, bison became the primary large game animal.

The way of life of Iowa's first inhabitants during the Paleo-Indian period is assumed to have been that of the nomadic, game hunter. From various sites outside the state we know that Paleo-Indian hunters often worked together to drive herds of bison over embankments or trapped them in steep-sided arroyos where they could more easily be killed and then butchered. In addition to the spearpoints so typical at Paleo-Indian sites, other artifacts include knives, scrapers, abraders, choppers, rubbing stones and some bone artifacts. Most of these can be seen to relate directly to the processing of game and the dressing of hides. Although almost nothing is known of the social organization, housing or more perishable artifacts of Paleo-Indian people like clothing, it is assumed that social interaction necessary for driving and killing herds of game would have involved cooperation among hunters and an established pattern of social control. Housing would probably have been temporary, involving some form of branch or bone frame with a covering of skins or mats. Clothes likewise would have been made of skins. Unfortunately, these are the kinds of items which are not usually preserved, and so we are left to speculate about them.

REFERENCES

Agogino, F. & W. D. Frankforter
1960   A Paleo-Indian Bison Kill in Northwestern Iowa. **American Antiquity,** Vol. 25: 414-415.

Alex, Lynn Marie
1976   Paleo-Indian Period. Office of the State Archaeologist Educational Series I. Iowa City.

Anderson, Adrian & Joseph Tiffany
1972 Rummels-Maske: A Clovis Find Spot in Iowa. **Plains Anthropologist** Vol. 17: 55-59.

Anderson, Duane
1975 **Western Iowa Prehistory.** Ames: Iowa State University Press.

Anderson, Duane & Richard Shutler, Jr.
1979 The Cherokee Sewer Site (13CK405): A Summary and Assessment. **Plains Anthropologist Memoir** 14.

Brown, Lionel
1967 Pony Creek Archaeology. **Publication in Salvage Archaeology, 5.** Smithsonian Institution River Basin Surveys: 65-72.

Frankforter, W. D.
1959 A Pre-Ceramic Site in Western Iowa. **Journal of the Iowa Archeological Society,** Vol. 8 (4): 47-72.

Frankforter, W. D. & George A. Agogino
1959 Archaic and Paleo-Indian Archaeological Discoveries in Western Iowa. **Texas Journal of Science,** Vol. 11 (4): 482-91.

Frankforter, W. D. & George A. Agogino
1960 The Simonsen Site: Report for the Summer of 1959. **Plains Anthropologist,** Vol. 5 (10): 65-70.

McKusick, Marshall
1964 **Men of Ancient Iowa.** Ames: Iowa State University Press.

Rowe, P. R.
1952 Early Horizons in Mills County Iowa. **Journal of the Iowa Archeological Society,** Vol. 1 (3): 6-13; Vol. 2 (1): 3-9.

Shutler, Richard, Duane C. Anderson **et. al.**
1974 Preliminary Report of a Stratified Paleo-Indian/Archaic Site in Northwestern Iowa. **Journal of the Iowa Archeological Society,** Vol. 21.

Chapter 10

Archaic Period

The Archaic Period in Iowa refers to prehistoric remains which occur after those of the Paleo-Indian between 8,500 and 1,000 years ago. Archaic materials have been found widely scattered across the state as surface discoveries and at a number of excavated archaeological sites, particularly in the western part of Iowa. The most characteristic artifacts of the Archaic are projectile points, especially medium-sized, triangular-shaped points, often with a concave base and notches on each side or at the corners to facilitate hafting them to the shaft. Frequently both the base and notches have been ground (dulled) so that the material used to bind them would not be cut by a sharp edge. Within this category there is considerable variation in points across the state. Other typical chipped stone artifacts include several different forms of scrapers, ovoid blades, drills and notched flakes.

Ground stone tools, a new category of stone artifact, also make their appearance in Iowa during this time. The pecking and grinding processes involved in the production of ground stone tools allowed for the use of harder, less easily worked stone such as granite and quartzite which was made into tools for grinding, crushing and chopping. Typical ground stone tools from the Iowa Archaic include abraders, axes, manos, and metates.

Nuts and seeds were ground
by Archaic peoples using
a mano and metate

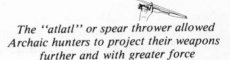

*The "atlatl" or spear thrower allowed
Archaic hunters to project their weapons
further and with greater force*

The presence of ground stone bannerstones in Archaic sites in eastern Iowa suggests the invention of a new hunting device — the atlatl. The atlatl was a composite tool usually consisting of a wooden shaft about two feet long fitted with a hook of antler at one end and a handle at the other. Perforated shell weights, or bannerstone weights, would also have been fitted onto the wooden shaft. By using an atlatl, Archaic hunters would have been able to throw their darts further and with greater force than before.

A number of bone artifacts were also made by Archaic peoples. Bone awls probably used for a variety of tasks such as piercing skins or working basket fibers are found. Bone scraping tools are known. And, at the Cherokee Sewer Site in Cherokee County, a flute made from the hollow bone of a bird was discovered. It is believed to be the earliest artifact of

A bird bone flute from the Cherokee Sewer site

A copper awl, one of the many copper objects known from Iowa sites

its kind in North America. We also know that it was during the Archaic that people in North America began to hammer chunks of raw copper from deposits in the Great Lakes region into a variety of artifacts. These were then traded widely throughout eastern North America. A copper pin, possibly acquired in trade, was found at the Olin Site in eastern Iowa and probably dates to the Archaic.

A number of excavated sites in Iowa, like the upper level (Horizon I) at the Cherokee Sewer Site, the Simonsen Site in Cherokee County, and a site near Pisgah in Harrison County, have been interpreted as places where bison were killed by Archaic hunters. In the lowest level excavated at the Simonsen Site, numerous bison bones were found, suggesting that Archaic hunters had killed and butchered at least 25 animals. Hunting of large game was thus an important part of the economy. Nevertheless, as is the case with Archaic sites outside Iowa, there is evidence that smaller animals were becoming increasingly important. The remains of deer, elk, wolf, rodent, fish, turtle, bird and shell-fish have been found at Archaic sites. There was also a growing reliance on plants, especially wild seeds and nuts. At the Simonsen Site and the Cherokee Sewer Site hackberry seeds were recovered, and at the latter site, the remains of goosefoot and hickory nuts were also present.

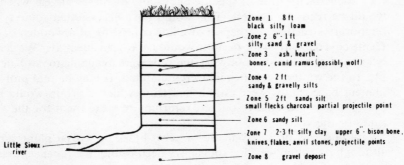

A profile of the Simonsen site shows how the cultural layers were found stratified, one over the other. The oldest layers are at the bottom, the youngest (most recent) occur above

The Archaic is characterized by an explosion in technological innovation. This seems to reflect an increasing ability on the part of Archaic communities to utilize natural resources. Undoubtedly this relates to the wider variety of plants and animals available in certain, milder, Post-Pleistocene environments, particularly the woodlands of eastern Iowa. We can expect that in the west, where more open conditions prevailed and where big game hunting continued as the primary subsistence activity, there were fewer discernible changes in lifestyle.

Because of the larger number of excavated sites, we know a good deal more about the Archaic way of life than we did about that of the Paleo-Indian. A number of sites such as the Lungren and Hill sites in Mills County, the Ocheyedan Site in Osceola County, and the Soldow Site in Humboldt County, appear to represent the remains of small campsites. Here, artifacts, broken animal bones and flint chips were found intermingled and surrounding hearths where small groups of Archaic peoples camped. The presence of flint chips suggests that stone artifacts were made and repaired at the camp. Many of the artifacts from the Cherokee Sewer Site were manufactured of stone which comes from some distance from the site. This suggests that chunks of stone were brought from a source to the camp and then manufactured into tools. The majority of the artifacts from these camps are stone and bone tools for butchering meat and dressing hides, two important activities to Archaic peoples. Since pottery is unknown in Archaic sites, it is probable that some cooking was carried out by heating stones in the hearth and dropping them into skin bags or tightly woven baskets filled with water. Meat was then added to the container and cooked in the hot water. Piles of burned rocks are sometimes found near the hearth suggesting this practice.

We have little concrete evidence of the type of houses that were built or the clothing worn, but we can infer something about these aspects of Archaic life. The pattern of residence would most likely have been migratory with small groups of families moving about as the seasons changed and as different food resources became available. It is likely that Archaic people, though mobile, traveled within familiar territories where they knew the location of specific plants and the times of year when they would be ready to harvest. This would have necessitated some type of temporary structure. Perhaps a dwelling consisting of a wooden or bone frame covered with skins or mats would have been adequate. We certainly know that hide and woodworking tools were available to Archaic people. In the winter, rockshelters were inhabited. It may be that more permanent base camps were established from which a group would move out to collect seasonal resources, returning to store them for the leaner times of the year.

Clothing was probably made of sewn hides or woven plant fabrics, although no actual weaving tools have been found in Archaic sites in the state. As with the Paleo-Indian peoples, social groups would probably have remained small, perhaps consisting of a few families who cooperated with one another particularly in food-getting activities. We suspect that the overall population level in Iowa towards the end of the Archaic had increased over Paleo-Indian times.

We know something of the burial customs of Archaic people as a result of excavations at the Lewis Central School Site in Pottawattomie

County, and at the Turin Site in Monona County. The Lewis Central School Site represented a Late Archaic ossuary, where eleven individuals had been buried. While a number of utilitarian items of bone and stone had been placed with the dead, there was no evidence that these artifacts or the bodies themselves had been arranged in any special way. In contrast, the older, Middle Archaic Turin Site, shows a greater concern for the comforts of the deceased. Here, four burials were discovered consisting of an adult male, an adolescent, a child, and an infant. All were found placed in a flexed position, their knees raised to their chests, and lying on their sides. The adolescent had been placed in a shallow grave and red ochre (a powdered form of iron oxide) had been sprinkled over the body. Placed with this individual was a necklace of shell beads (perhaps a symbol of status) and a side-notched projectile point similar to those from the Simonsen Site 40 miles away. It seems evident from these burials that Archaic people took care in the disposal of their dead, placing with them personal, and perhaps to them, valuable items. In the prehistoric world the dead were often covered with red ochre, for what reasons we can only guess. The burial of the young person at Turin was not unlike the burial of people in Europe or the Near East who lived during the same time period.

Several of the western Iowa sites with Archaic materials, particularly the Hill, Simonsen, and Cherokee Sewer sites, have been compared to other Plains Archaic sites like the Logan Creek site in eastern Nebraska. Marshall McKusick, in *Men of Ancient Iowa,* has suggested grouping all of these into what he calls the "Logan Creek Complex" (a complex being a group of sites which have the same range of tool types). This complex consists of both kill sites and small campsites. Prairie Archaic projectile points, ovoid blades and a variety of scrapers including notched end scrapers are characteristic finds. A number of ground stone tools also occur at Logan Creek, Hill, and the Cherokee Sewer Site. Other excavated sites with similar types would include the Lungren Site, Turin, and the Pisgah Site. Similar materials have been found as surface discoveries at a site on the Keg Creek floodplain of the east branch of the Des Moines River in Humboldt County. In addition to a small number of Paleo-Indian type projectile points, this site produced Archaic-type, side-

A bison jump — Archaic people killed large numbers of bison by stampeding them over cliffs. Men and women lined up to form a V-shaped trap into which the bison were driven. Shouting and waving blankets and firebrands, the hunters sent the terrified animals over the cliff edge to their death at the foot of the jump.

notched points and side-notched end scrapers. Similar artifacts have been reported from surface collections in the central Des Moines river valley.

Although well-defined Archaic complexes from excavated sites in eastern Iowa are virtually unknown at this time, such materials are frequently encountered as surface finds. In addition, a small number of Archaic types occur in the lower levels of many rock shelters in the eastern part of the state. One intriguing eastern site is the Olin Site on the Wapsipinicon River in Jones County. Here, dredging operations recovered faunal remains of bison, beaver, and caribou together with a copper pin and Osceola type points from a depth of 35 feet. Although the status of this site remains a mystery, a comparison with similar materials in the Old Copper Culture of Wisconsin is suggested. This is reinforced by surface finds from northeast Iowa of other side-notched projectile points and copper artifacts resembling those from the Old Copper Osceola Site in Wisconsin.

The Archaic of Iowa suggests a general affinity with sites on a similar time level elsewhere in North America. Specific parallels have been noted between western Iowa sites and the Logan Creek and Spring Creek sites in Nebraska. The western Iowa sites in general share many similarities with other Archaic sites in the Plains-Prairie area. On the other hand, there is some suggestion that sites in the eastern part of the state are more closely related to those like Modoc Rock Shelter in Illinois, Graham Cave in Missouri, and the Wisconsin Archaic sites. It may be that in eastern Iowa the more extensive woodland environment brought about a cultural adaptation different from that of the more open environment of the Plains-Prairie region.

REFERENCES

Alex, Lynn Marie
1976   Archaic Period. **Office of the State Archaeologist Educational Series 2.** Iowa City.

Anderson, Duane
1975   **Western Iowa Prehistory.** Ames: Iowa State University Press.

Anderson, Duane C. and Richard Shutler, Jr.
1979   The Cherokee Sewer Site (13CK405): A Summary and Assessment. **Plains Anthropologist Memoir** 14, pp. 132-139.

Anderson, Duane **et. al.**
1978   The Lewis Central School Site (13PW5): A Resolution of Ideological Conflicts at an Archaic Ossuary in Western Iowa. **Plains Anthropologist,** Vol. 23 (81): 183-219.

Flanders, Richard
1977   The Soldow Site: An Archaic Component from North Central Iowa. **Journal of the Iowa Archeological Society,** Vol. 24: 125-147.

Frankforter, W. D.
1961 Meaning of Archaic and Possible Relationships. **Journal of the Iowa Archeological Society.** Vol. 10 (4): 26-31.

Jennings, Jesse
1968 **Prehistory of North America.** New York: McGraw-Hill.

McKusick, Marshall
1964 **Men of Ancient Iowa.** Ames: Iowa State University Press.

Ruppe, Reynold
1954 An Archaic Site at Olin, Iowa. **Journal of the Iowa Archeological Society,** Vol. 3 (4): 12-15.

Shutler, Richard, Duane Anderson, **et. al.**
1974 Preliminary Report of a Stratified Paleo-Indian/Archaic Site in Northwestern Iowa. **Journal of the Iowa Archeological Society,** Vol. 21.

Chapter 11

Woodland Period

The transition from the Archaic Period to what has traditionally been called the Woodland occurs in some parts of the U.S. by about 3000 B.P. In theory, the Woodland is characterized by the appearance of three new traits: pottery, burial mounds, and cultivated plants. Ideally, it is these three characteristics which separate the cultures of the Woodland from those of the Archaic.

If we look at any particular area of the U.S. after this time, we find that there are problems in applying this definition of the Woodland. While there is evidence that these three traits spread across much of the U.S. east of the Rocky Mountains, they were not accepted at the same time nor by all societies. In some areas, two of these traits, horticulture and burial mounds, appear at sites many archaeologists would call Archaic. For instance, in eastern Iowa the Turkey River Mounds of Clayton County, which date about 3000 B.P., contain burials covered with red ochre (iron oxide) and a variety of grave goods such as Turkey Tail and straight-stemmed projectile points, and cylindrical copper beads, but no pottery. They are called Archaic by some archaeologists and Woodland by others.

It is possible the people who built the Turkey River Mounds and other "Red Ochre" mounds in northeastern Iowa made the earliest known ceramics in the state, but if they did we have no evidence of it. For most archaeologists, the appearance of pottery marks the beginning of the Early Woodland Period in Iowa.

The very first potters of the Early Woodland Period may have copied the shape and design of their pots from basketry or leather containers. These first vessels tend to be thick, straight-walled, flat-bottomed pots with large amounts of grit or sometimes fiber temper. The earliest known type of pottery in Iowa is Marion Thick. Marion Thick has been found at habitation sites in the eastern part of the state, such as the Elephant Terrace Site in northern Allamakee County. Other sites containing this early type of pottery are also found in the eastern part of Iowa, particularly in the valley of the Mississippi River and its tributaries.

At sites somewhat later in time than those containing Marion Thick pottery, there occurs a second type of Early Woodland ceramic, Black Sand pottery. Sites containing Black Sand pottery are often found on sand ridges in the valley bottoms of large rivers in eastern Iowa such as the Mississippi, the lower Skunk, and the lower Iowa. Black Sand pottery is somewhat better made than Marion Thick and contains cord or fabric markings on the exterior surface only. The people who made Black Sand pottery incised or scratched designs of lines, triangles, and dashes onto the surface of the wet clay before the pot was fired using a pointed bone or wooden tool. Spring Hollow Incised pottery, which is found along the prairie streams in eastern, central, and northern Iowa, is almost indistinguishable from Black Sand, but may be later in time.

In the Central Illinois River Valley and the adjacent valley of the Mississippi River we find the development of a Middle Woodland ceramic tradition called Havana. This tradition eventually spread as far west as Oklahoma and the Missouri River Valley of southwestern Iowa. The Middle Woodland Period in parts of Iowa begins about A.D. 1 with the appearance of large village sites containing Havana pottery such as the Yellow River Village, Kingston, and Wolfe sites. While some of these habitation sites have been excavated, most of the interest in the Middle Woodland has centered on mound exploration, much of which was conducted by the Davenport Academy of Sciences in the late nineteenth century. These Middle Woodland Mounds fall within the well-known Hopewellian Complex. Hopewell represents one in a series of mortuary traditions which existed in the eastern U.S. between 3000 B.P. and the time of historic contact with Europeans. Although sometimes referred to as a culture, Hopewell was probably more of a burial or mortuary cult, which spread over a wide area and was superimposed on local, regionally distinct Middle Woodland cultures.

Hopewellian sites are most characteristically cemeteries of mounds often containing multiple burials placed inside or outside log tombs. Some of the burials in these mounds are cremations while others are inhumations sometimes with stone slabs covering the bodies. With the burial were placed elaborate artifacts which frequently incorporated exotic raw materials such as Golf Coast conch shell, obsidian from the Rocky Mountains, Appalachian mica, and Great Lakes copper. Such items suggest that the people with whom they were buried may have held a position of high social status within the society, one which allowed them access to these luxury goods. They also suggest the existence of an elaborate trade network which stretched over a wide geographical territory. The similarity of items found accompanying burials, as well as the exotic raw materials, suggest that societies participated in frequent interaction with groups thousands of miles away. While local traditions in pottery-making and manufacture of chipped stone tools continued, burial artifacts such as mortuary pottery, ceramic and finely carved stone pipes, human and animal figurines, stone and copper axes, panpipes, and finely chipped flint, chert, and obsidian projectile points are duplicated in sites from Iowa to New York and from Wisconsin to Florida.

A Hopewell Pipe

Exotic materials may have been traded over long distances during Woodland times

Mound groups such as those at Toolesboro in Louisa County and the Cook Farm Group in present-day Davenport, are certain evidence of the extension of Hopewell into Iowa. Related mound groups in northeastern Iowa provide additional confirmation of Iowa's participation in funerary traditions and long-distance trade with societies throughout the eastern U.S. These trade routes were undoubtably the mechanism whereby exotic goods and ideas reached Iowa. The rituals and beliefs associated with the Hopewell Cult were probably transmitted along with mortuary items. Further west, there is much less evidence of any participation in Hopewellian traditions although trade items did find their way into this area. In east-central Iowa, locally made Cedar Ware is likely a native imitation of Havana ceramics. Middle Woodland Rowe Ware from the Glenwood area of southwestern Iowa, shows a blend of influences from the Havana tradition and from Plains ceramics.

A.D. 500 is a convenient date for separating the Middle Woodland Period from the Late Woodland Period in Iowa. By this time, the large Havana villages of southeastern Iowa were replaced by smaller, less sedentary Woodland campsites. Mounds are still being used as monuments to the dead, but they are smaller and lack most of the exotic trade items found in the Hopewellian mounds. Late Woodland mounds were not confined to the generally conical shape of most of Iowa's Middle Woodland mounds; they are commonly oblong (linear) and in northeastern Iowa were frequently made into the shape of animals. These animal-shaped or "effigy" mounds are found primarily in Allamakee and Clayton counties although they extend as far south as the city of Dubuque.

The Marching Bear Effigy Mounds

Cord-wrapped stick decorated vessel from a conical mound in Clayton County.

The bag-shaped pottery of Early and Middle Woodland sites gives way to more rounded vessels by Late Woodland times. Linn Ware (analogous to Illinois Weaver Ware), and Madison and Minnott's fabric impressed wares are common ceramics of the Late Woodland in eastern Iowa sites. They are comparable to pottery types in Illinois and Wisconsin. Again, western Iowa pottery, including Sterns Creek types and Missouri Bluffs Cord Impressed, reflect a stronger affiliation with those from Late Woodland sites on the Plains.

While a number of Woodland habitation sites have been excavated, such as the Keystone and Hadfield rock shelters in eastern Iowa, we know far less about the type of houses built by Woodland peoples and much more about the mounds they erected about their dead. The basic social unit was probably the immediate family. Larger social groups may have formed during certain seasons of the year when native plants and animals were abundant. Dr. R. Clark Mallam has suggested, in fact, that the Effigy Mounds and related mounds of Allamakee and Clayton counties were constructed not only as refuges for the dead, but also to mark territorial boundaries between groups and to strengthen social ties. Perhaps the mounds were ceremonial centers which acted to draw people together for a common purpose on certain occasions.

Although we know that some plants were cultivated by Woodland people elsewhere in North America, we have no good evidence of this in Woodland sites in Iowa. In fact, limited evidence now available suggests that natural resources, wild plants and animals, were particularly abundant in Woodland times. This would have been especially true in areas such as eastern Iowa where several diverse microenvironments came in contact. Some plants such as pigweed, wild rice, arrowleaf, and yellow lotus, may have provided important surpluses in the economy of Woodland peoples. An abundant surplus could have allowed some Woodland groups to become more sedentary. The large Middle Woodland villages of southeastern Iowa may reflect such a situation.

A variety of stemmed, corner and side notched dart points were used by Iowa hunters in the Woodland period.

The use of the spear or dart in hunting seems to have continued throughout the Woodland Period. Points resembling Raddatz Side-notched, Turkey Tail, Waubesa Contracting Stem and Snyders types as well as a variety of other stemmed, corner, and side-notched forms have been found in Iowa in early to Middle Woodland contexts. However, by Late Woodland times, the bow and arrow were being used. This is suggested by the occurrence of smaller, notched and unnotched, triangular-shaped points.

After about A.D. 900 we see for a time the persistence of some Late Woodland cultures. However, the adaptation to a horticultural economy, the acceptance of new styles of ceramics, and perhaps an actual influx of outside populations brought about an end to the traditional Woodland pattern in Iowa. By A.D. 1000 we are able to identify a number of distinct late prehistoric cultures in the states. These groups were largely horticultural although they retained some of the features of the Woodland cultures that preceded them.

REFERENCES

Alex, Lynn Marie
1976   Woodland. Office of the State Archaeologist Educational Series 3. Iowa City.

Anderson, Adrian
1971   Review of Iowa River Valley Archaeology, in Prehistoric Investigations, Marshall McKusick (ed.). **Office of the State Archaeologist, Report #3.** Iowa City.

Anderson, Duane
1975   **Western Iowa Prehistory.** Ames: Iowa State University Press.

Benn, David
1976   The Woodland Cultures of Northeast Iowa (A.D. 300-800): A Perspective from Hadfields Cave Site. Doctoral dissertation, **University Microfilms,** University of Michigan, Ann Arbor.

Benn, David and Dean Thompson
1977   The Young Site, Linn County, Iowa and Comments on Woodland Ceramics. **Journal of the Iowa Archeological Society,** Vol. 24: 1-61.

Flanders, Richard and Rex Hansman
1961   A Woodland Mound Complex in Webster County, Iowa. **Journal of the Iowa Archeological Society,** Vol. 11 (1): 1-12.

Herold, Elaine Bluhm
1970   Hopewell: Burial Mound Builders. **Palimpsest** 51 (12): 497-528.

Jennings, Jesse
1968   **Prehistory of North America.** New York: McGraw-Hill

Lass, Barbara
1978   The Woodland Mounds and their Cultural Significance. **Journal of the Iowa Archeological Society,** Vol. 25: 101-113.

Logan, Wilford
1976   Woodland Complexes in Northeastern Iowa. **U.S. Dept. of the Interior National Park Service Publications in Archaeology,** 15. Washington, D.C.

Mallam, R. Clark
1976   The Iowa Effigy Mound Manifestation: An Interpretive Model. **Office of the State Archaeologist Report 9.** Iowa City.

McKusick, Marshall
1964   **Men of Ancient Iowa.** Ames: Iowa State University Press.

Orr, Ellison
1963   Iowa Archaeological Reports 1934-1939 (ten volumes) with an Evaluation and Index by Marshall McKusick. **Archives of Archaeology #20.**

Straffin, Dean
1971   Wolfe Havana Hopewell Site, in Prehistoric Investigations, Marshall McKusick (ed.). **Office of the State Archaeologist,** Report #3. Iowa City.

Tiffany, Joseph
1978   Middle Woodland Pottery Typology from Southwest Iowa. **Plains Anthropologist** 23 (81): 169-182.

Chapter 12

Great Oasis

During the late prehistoric period, western Iowa was inhabited by groups of people whose culture archaeologists refer to as "Great Oasis." Great Oasis remains were first discovered in southwestern Minnesota at the Low Village and Big Slough sites. We now know that the distribution of Great Oasis materials is quite extensive throughout the eastern periphery of the Plains. In addition to southwestern Minnesota, sites are found in eastern Nebraska, in Iowa in the vicinity of the Big and Little Sioux rivers and the Des Moines River drainage, and along the Missouri River as far west as Chamberlain, South Dakota. Isolated finds of Great Oasis artifacts in Iowa have been reported from the Coralville Reservoir and from the Glenwood vicinity in the southwestern part of the state. Archaeologists believe that environmental conditions or pressure from resident populations may have prevented Great Oasis people from expanding into other areas of Iowa.

Great Oasis is an early representative of the Plains Village Pattern which also includes the Mill Creek Cultures of western Iowa, the Over Focus sites of South Dakota, and Cambria, a site in southern Minnesota. Great Oasis is thought to have developed from a Woodland Culture base by A.D. 900. Some archaeologists believe that Great Oasis was ancestral to cultures like Mill Creek and Over Focus, but this relationship has not been confirmed. We know that Great Oasis sites date as late as the fourteenth century A.D. and are thus contemporary with other cultures of the Plains Village Pattern. For this reason, some archaeologists prefer to interpret the relationship between Mill Creek and Great Oasis as one of contemporary cultures rather than as one of ancestry. At the Broken Kettle Site in Plymouth County, a Great Oasis village was found right across the creek from a Mill Creek settlement. If two such different cultures coexisted side by side, their relationship may have been analogous to rural areas of Iowa today, where the Amish practice a more archaic lifestyle right next to their modern mechanized farming neighbors.

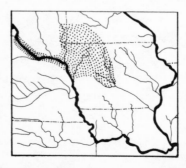

Great Oasis sites are distributed throughout northwestern Iowa and into surrounding areas.

The distribution of known sites indicates that Great Oasis people built their villages on low ground, usually on terraces above the floodplain of a nearby river or stream. A number of these sites in Iowa have been excavated including the Broken Kettle West Site and the Williams Site in Plymouth County, the Beals Site in Cherokee County, the Gypsum Quarry Site in Webster County, and portions of the Hubby, Meehan-Schell and Old Moser sites in Boone County. These excavations provide some idea of the type of houses and internal characteristics of Great Oasis villages. Houses like the four uncovered at the Broken Kettle West Site were long rectangular structures which had been built into a shallow pit about one and a half feet deep. House walls were constructed of vertical posts interwoven with sticks and plastered with mud. This is sometimes referred to as "wattle and daub" construction. From small amounts of burned thatch found in the excavation, archaeologists were able to infer that the roofs of these structures were composed of grass thatching and probably built in the form of a rounded dome. A covered entryway extended outward from the narrow end of the house.

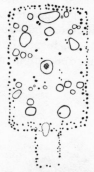

The floor plan of a Great Oasis structure.

Within each of these structures, a central fireplace and many trash and cache (storage) pits had been constructed. We know from historic accounts of people like the Mandan and Hidatsa that cache pits were designed to keep food and other items. Once their contents had spoiled or were disturbed by rodents however, they would be emptied. Since it was dangerous to have a large, open pit on the house floor, the inhabitants would fill the empty pits with rubbish. When archaeologists excavate such pits they often find an abundance of broken pottery, discarded stone and bone tools, chipped stone flakes, and animal and plant remains. It is possible to analyze these remains in order to retrieve information about the diet of Great Oasis people and to discern the time of year that the house was occupied. In one of the Broken Kettle West houses, cache pits contained the remains of large mammals such as deer, elk, bison, wolf, and coyote as well as smaller forms like rabbit, gopher, mouse, mole, frog, turtle, snake and a variety of birds and fish. From the quantity of deer and elk bone, it appeared that these were the two most important animals hunted. In fact, evidence from other Great Oasis sites suggests that these may have been more important than bison. Seeds of corn, sunflower, and squash or gourd indicated the garden crops cultivated; while the remains of goosefoot, pigweed, clover, smartweed, pondweed, hackberry, and walnut pointed to types of wild plants collected.

It has been suggested that Great Oasis people lived in large, permanent villages during certain times of the year, but that during the summer they left the village for a communal bison hunt or split into small groups to establish garden plots at other locations. Broken Kettle West may be an example of one of the larger more permanent Great Oasis villages. Here the animal remains from cache pits suggested that the site was occupied throughout the fall, winter, and spring months. An analysis of the seasonal growth rings on fish scales pointed to the fall occupation; a deer skull with antlers shed suggested residence during the winter months; a bird's medullary bone, which appears only during the reproductive period, was evidence that the inhabitants had occupied the site during the spring. The Williams Site, in contrast, may help to explain the whereabouts of Great Oasis people during the summer. Here, the small size of the site and its shallow deposits suggested a short-term occupation. The abundance of corn and other seeds indicated that gardening was an important activity to the residents. It may be that the Williams Site represents one of the small summer encampments of Great Oasis people.

An artist's reconstruction of a Great Oasis house blends architectural knowledge with archaeological evidence. Post mold patterns in the floor of the structure indicate the general shape and layout of the wall plan. Pieces of wall daub and burned thatching found in the excavation suggest the materials used in wall and roof construction.

Stone tools used by Great Oasis people are similar to those of other Plains cultures although certain anomalies exist. The bow and arrow, which had replaced the spear used by earlier groups, is represented by numerous small triangular projectile points. A lingering Woodland characteristic seems to exist in the presence of stemmed, corner-notched points found at some sites. Many of the chipped stone tools are made of materials which must have been traded in from sources at some distance from the site. Bijou Hills quartzite and Knife River flint, which occur in Great Oasis contexts, are two stone types whose sources lie outside the state.

Although the remains of domesticated plants in sites indicate that Great Oasis people were horticulturists, there are almost no examples of manos, metates, or scapula hoes. These are common gardening implements in other Plains sites and their absence is surprising. It may be that Great Oasis people used other types of tools for gardening or traded with other cultures for their garden produce.

Perhaps the most distinctive of Great Oasis artifacts are ceramics including Great Oasis High Rim and Great Oasis Wedge Lip wares. The presence of a smoothed-over-cordmarked surface on some Great Oasis vessels is a typical Woodland trait and is another characteristic which suggests the derivation of Great Oasis from a Woodland Culture base.

Although the remains of human bone are occasionally found in village refuse, most Great Oasis cemeteries appear to be located on hill or bluff top locations away from the living area. It appears that Great Oasis people practiced a number of different burial customs including both interment (sometimes in a mound) and cremation. Both single and multiple burials have been found. We know of one extensive Great Oasis cemetery in the city of West Des Moines where the remains of 18 individuals were found. These people had been buried in a flexed position (knees drawn up to their chest), and were accompanied by a number of grave items including hundreds of small *Anculosa* (a type of snail) shell beads and eight crosses manufactured from clam shell.

The exact relationship between Great Oasis people and contemporary groups is not precisely known. There is abundant evidence, however, that trade was established over long distances. Gulf Coast conch and *Anculosa* shell beads from the Ohio and Arkansas river valleys are found in some Great Oasis sites and confirm the presence of a widespread trading network to the south and east. We do not know what products were exchanged by great Oasis people for these exotic items. Some archaeologists have suggested that foodstuffs, such as meat, or skins may have been traded to outside groups. Unfortunately, these are highly perishable items which rarely survive in the archaeological record.

REFERENCES

Alex, Lynn Marie
1976   Great Oasis. **Office of the State Archaeologist Educational Series 7.** Iowa City.

Anderson, Duane
1975   **Western Iowa Prehistory.** Ames: Iowa State University Press.

Baerreis, David **et. al.**
1970   Environmental Archaeology in Western Iowa. **Northwest Chapter of the Iowa Archeological Society Newsletter,** Vol. 18 (5): 3-5.

Gradwohl, David
1974   Archaeology of the Central Des Moines River Valley, in Aspects of Upper Great Lakes Anthropology, Papers in Honor of Lloyd Wilford, **Minnesota Prehistoric Archaeology Series** #11: 90-102.

Henning, Dale R.
1967   Mississippian Influences on the Eastern Plains Border: An Evaluation. **Plains Anthropologist,** Vol. 12 (36): 184-194.

Henning, Dale R.
1971   Great Oasis Culture Distributions, in Prehistoric Investigations, Marshall McKusick (ed.). **Office of the State Archaeologist, Report #3.** Iowa City.

Johnson, Elden
1969   Decorative Motifs on Great Oasis Pottery. **Plains Anthropologist,** Vol. 14 (46): 272-276.

Johnston, Richard B.
1967   The Hitchell Site. **Publications in Salvage Archaeology, No. 3, Smithsonian Institution River Basin Surveys.**

Knauth, Otto
1963   Mystery of the Crosses. **Annals of Iowa,** Vol. 37 (2): 81-91.

McKusick, Marshall
1964   **Men of Ancient Iowa.** Ames: Iowa State University Press.

Wilford, Lloyd
1945   Three villages of the Mississippian Pattern in Minnesota. **American Antiquity,** Vol. 11 (1): 32-40.

Williams, Patricia McAlister
1975   The Williams Site (13PM50): A Great Oasis Component in Northwest Iowa. **Journal of the Iowa Archeological Society,** Vol. 22: 1-34.

Chapter 13

Mill Creek

In northwestern Iowa and along the tributaries of the Missouri River in South and North Dakota, a series of archaeological cultures occur which represent the remains of compact villages of sedentary horticulturists. These cultures have been grouped by archaeologists into what is called the Middle Missouri Tradition. In Iowa, this tradition is represented by the Mill Creek Culture. Mill Creek sites occur in northwestern Iowa on terraces above the Big Sioux River and its tributary Broken Kettle Creek in Plymouth County, and along the Little Sioux River and its tributaries Mill Creek and Waterman Creek in Cherokee, O'Brien, and Buena Vista counties.

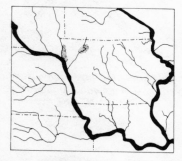

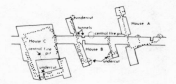

Mill Creek house plans recovered at the Kimball site.

Distribution of Mill Creek sites in northwest Iowa.

Mill Creek sites consist of large mounds, sometimes 10 to 12 feet deep, which may extend for as much as an acre. These mounds have formed as a result of the accumulation of village refuse perhaps over a considerable period of time. In some cases, the remains of as many as three houses have been found superimposed over each other.

Evidence from the Kimball Site in Plymouth County, suggests that some Mill Creek houses were arranged in an orderly row. At other sites, such as Chan-ya-ta in Buena Vista County, a more haphazard arrangement is indicated. Each house was a semi-subterranean earthlodge with an entryway at one end. Vertical timber posts were connected with a lattice work (wattle) of small branches and plastered with grass-tempered mud (daub) to form the walls. We are not sure of the arrangement of the timber posts which supported the roof, but it would not appear to have been the four central roof supports found in houses of the Central Plains Tradition.

As in other Plains village houses, the floors of Mill Creek structures were dotted with large basin and bell-shaped cache pits. Cache pits also occur outside of the house. The prolific number of bone tools, pottery, and charred plant remains found in Mill Creek cache pits suggests that these people were successful horticulturists who maintained garden plots

133

of corn, beans, squash, pumpkin and sunflower. The prairie sod of the Midwest is characterized by grasses which have a tough, thick root system which is almost impossible to cultivate without the use of the modern steel plow. Thus, prior to the European settlement, Native American horticulturists farmed the loose, rich, river bottomland using bone hoes made from the scapula or skull of large mammals and bone or wooden digging sticks. These hoes are a common item in Mill Creek sites and were most frequently manufactured from the scapula of a bison. The scapula was also used to make a blunt-ended knife which had a straight edge on one side and a convex-concave edge on the other. This was probably used in the processing of garden produce as were similar knives in historic times.

Cross section of a historic Hidatsa cache pit
(after Lowie, 1954).

Scapula hoes may have been hafted to
a forked shaft in a manner similar to those
of the Hidatsa.

The presence of this abundant bone industry points to hunting as another important activity in the Mill Creek economy. According to the evidence at some sites, Mill Creek people probably abandoned their village at certain times of the year to hunt. While smaller game, fish, and birds may well have been caught throughout the year by individual hunters, bison were most likely hunted communally at certain specific times. For instance, once crops were planted in the early summer, a communal bison hunt could take place with most of the able-bodied population participating. Some members might have remained in the village to care for the crops, the aged, and the very young children, but most would be out on the hunt. Animals would be killed with bow and small, side-notched projectile points. Butchering probably occurred at the kill site, and certain chunks of meat were brought back to the village dried, or to be dried, and stored for the winter ahead. We infer this practice from the fact that we find a higher percentage of certain specific parts of the bison in the village sites while other parts are consistently absent. These missing parts were probably eaten immediately after the kill or left at the butchering spot. A second bison hunt may have taken place later on in the year.

While we assume that many of the animal bones found at an archaeological site reflect the diet of prehistoric people, others were utilized for additional purposes. The bones of mammals, fish, and birds were made into a wide variety of items. Hide grainers, shaft straighteners, hoes, knives, sickles, and flaking tools were all utilitarian implements manufactured from the bone of bison, elk, and deer. Large catfish were caught by Mill Creek peoples using bone fishhooks. These hooks had a bulbous end on their shaft which probably made it easier to attach them to a line. Fine bone needles and pointed awls of bison or bird bone or the dorsal spine of the drum fish allowed Mill Creek people to sew skins and work basket fibers. Often these skins and baskets were decorated with flattened porcupine quills which had been worked with spatulate pieces of bone. *Anculosa* and conch shell beads, shell pendants, carved bone pins, and a variety of teeth including those of bear, dog, and beaver, used in decoration, were other items which Mill Creek people acquired as by-products of hunting.

In addition to bone tools and decorative ornaments, the skins and feathers of animals were incorporated into ceremonial items. The case of birds is a particularly interesting one. We know from ethnographic accounts of historic Plains groups, such as the Osage, Omaha, and Arikara, that medicine bundles composed of bird skin wrappings filled with sacred objects were used on ceremonial occasions. Stuffed bird skins also served as personal fetishes believed to bring good luck to their owners. In order to give some form to the bundle, the skull and bones of the wing and feet would be left attached to the skin. Although we are not certain of the existence of these bird bundles in prehistoric times, the occurrence of bones from the feet, wing, and skull of a bird found together in an archaeological site strongly suggests their existence.

Fishhooks are believed to have been manufactured from bone "blanks."

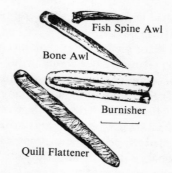

Fish Spine Awl

Bone Awl

Burnisher

Quill Flattener

Other ceremonial or decorative items manufactured from birds, such as bird headdresses, claws, and wing or tail fans, are also indicated by archaeological finds. At the Brewster Site in Cherokee County, the lower wing and foot bones of raptorial birds (hawks, eagles, falcons) were particularly abundant. This suggests that Mill Creek people were hunting or trapping such birds not necessarily for food but to be used in the manufacture of decorative and ceremonial objects.

The bones of animals utilized by Mill Creek people in Iowa in some cases represent species like the passenger pigeon, which have since become extinct or are no longer native to northwestern Iowa. At the Brewster Site and the Broken Kettle Site in Plymouth County, the remains of the river redhorse, a type of sucker, were recovered. As this fish has not been reported in Iowa since the turn of the century, and as it is a species which prefers clear stream conditions, we assume that the siltier nature of some of our modern streams has resulted in its disappearance from the state.

Mill Creek potters were equally skillful, manufacturing a wide variety of vessels including bowls, flat bottomed rectangular pans, seed jars, wide-mouthed bottles, hooded water bottles, jars and ollas (wide-mouthed water jars). Archaeologists have classified these into the four major Mill Creek wares described earlier: Sanford, Chamberlain, Foreman, and Mill Creek. The design motifs found on these wares are usually geometric patterns like rectangles and diamonds. More distinctive motifs include the so-called running deer and weeping eye. Some of the pots have loop handles or effigy handles representing small animals or birds.

The effigy handles on some Mill Creek vessels may have represented the totem animal of the potter's family. In societies where a newly married couple establishes their home with the wife's family, something called matrilocal residence, the crafts made by women such as pottery are very similar from generation to generation because daughters learn ceramic-making from their mothers, aunts, and grandmothers with whom they continue to live. Among historic Plains village people like the Mandan, communities were composed of several clans of related matrilineages, who were affiliated by a common ancestry through the female line. Matrilocal residence was also the rule among the Mandan. Archaeologists believe that Mill Creek villages were probably matrilocal and matrilineal because the ceramics in each settlement tend to remain uniform over time.

The origin of Mill Creek has been a puzzle to archaeologists for some time. It used to be thought that Mississippian people from the large urban center of Cahokia located in the Central Mississippi Valley in present East St. Louis, Illinois, had migrated to Iowa and became the ancestors of Mill Creek. There are a number of items found at Mill Creek sites which suggest connections with Cahokia. Features such as earspools (pulled-shaped stone or bone earrings), chunky stones (discoidal stones probably used in athletic games), elbow-shaped pipes, shell pendants, scalloped-edge shell gorgets, carved bone pins, the use of shell temper, *Anculosa* shell beads from the southern U.S. and marine shell traded from the Gulf of Mexico, are common to Mill Creek sites and to those in and around Cahokia. However, all of these items could have been acquired as a result of trade and the diffusion of ideas. Long distance contact along major rivers such as the Missouri, Mississippi and the Des Moines could explain the introduction of these items to Iowa.

It is doubtful that Mill Creek people had full-time traders or artisans, although some people may have been particularly adept at hunting, fishing, projectile point and ceramic making, storytelling and singing. What items Mill Creek people exchanged for the trade goods from Cahokia is not certain. It might have been the thick, luxurious bison robes acquired

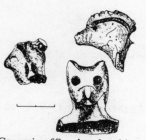

Ceramic effigy heads of human and animal form often decorate the rims of Mill Creek pottery.

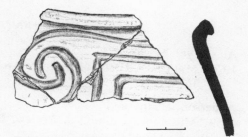

Evidence of contact between Mill Creek and Mississippian cultures is found in this Ramey Scroll, a frequent decorative motif on pottery at the prehistoric city of Cahokia.

in hunting, or a variety of bird feathers used in fans, headdresses and the like. Perhaps important families from Cahokia established alliances with prestigious Mill Creek lineages through marriage.

There is thus no conclusive evidence for the origin of Mill Creek in a migration of people from Cahokia. The lower levels (and presumably the oldest) at sites such as Phipps and Kimball indicate that Mill Creek was established by A.D. 900 and before the appearance of most of the Cahokia-related items. Most archaeologists today believe that Mill Creek represents a local development which was influenced by other cultures in Iowa and neighboring states, such as late Woodland, Great Oasis, the Over Focus of South Dakota, and Cahokia.

While Mill Creek people may have traded peacefully with other groups, there is reason to believe that not all of their contacts were friendly. At least three of the Mill Creek sites, Chan-ya-ta, the Double Ditch Site in O'Brien County, and Wittrock in O'Brien County were fortified with ditches on three sides. The fourth side faced the nearby stream so that these sites were protected on all four sides. At Wittrock, a log stockade had been constructed inside the ditch, and this may have been standard at other sites as well. One of the possible reasons for the disappearance of Mill Creek culture from Iowa prior to the arrival of Europeans was pressure from hostile groups, particularly Oneota. Oneota sites are contemporary with the later Mill Creek sites, and yet we find no Oneota items in Mill Creek contexts to suggest friendly trade or interaction.

Another important factor in the disappearance of Mill Creek was probably the climate. We know that about A.D. 1200-1250 the climate became drier and conditions for horticulture deteriorated. This may have put a strain on available timber resources so important for fuel and house construction. Faced with these conditions, Mill Creek people seem to have abandoned their villages and moved elsewhere.

It has been suggested that Mill Creek people gradually moved up the Missouri River and were incorporated in the late Over Focus of the Dakotas. Archaeologists believe that from such a tradition Siouan speaking groups such as the Mandan and Hidatsa developed. These people were living in large, permanent, earthlodge villages at the time of historic contact.

REFERENCES

Alex, Lynn Marie
1976   Mill Creek. **Office of the State Archaeologist Educational Series 4.** Iowa City.

Anderson, Duane
1969   Mill Creek Culture: A Review. **Plains Anthropologist,** Vol. 14 (44): 137-143.

Anderson, Duane
1972   The Ceramic Complex at the Brewster Site (13CK14): A Mill Creek Component in Northwestern Iowa. Doctoral Dissertation, **University Microfilms,** University of Michigan, Ann Arbor.

Anderson, Duane
1973   Brewster Site (13CK15): Lithic Analysis. **Journal of the Iowa Archeological Society,** Vol. 20: 1-75.

Anderson, Duane
1975   **Western Iowa Prehistory.** Ames: Iowa State University Press.

Flanders, Richard
1960   A Re-examination of Mill Creek Ceramics. The Robinson Technique. **Journal of the Iowa Archeological Society,** Vol. 10 (2): 1-34.

Fugle, Eugene
1962   Mill Creek Culture and Technology. **Journal of the Iowa Archeological Society,** Vol. 2 (4): 76-81.

Henning, Dale (ed.)
1968   Climatic Change and the Mill Creek Culture of Iowa, Part 1. **Journal of the Iowa Archeological Society,** Vol. 15.

Henning, Dale (ed.)
1971   Origins of Mill Creek. **Journal of the Iowa Archeological Society,** Vol. 18: 6-12.

Ives, John
1962   Mill Creek Pottery. **Journal of the Iowa Archeological Society.** Vol. 11 (3): 1-57.

Lehmer, Donald J.
1971   Introduction to Middle Missouri Archeology. **Anthropological Papers 1,** National Park Service, Department of the Interior. Washington.

Lowie, Robert
1954   **Indians of the Plains.** New York: McGraw-Hill.

McKusick, Marshall
1964   **Men of Ancient Iowa.** Ames: Iowa State University Press.

Scott, Donna Hurt
1979   Analysis of Avifauna from 5 Sites in Northwest Iowa. **Journal of the Iowa Archeological Society,** Vol. 26: 43-80.

Tiffany, Joseph A.
1978   A Model for Changing Settlement Patterns for the Mill Creek Culture of Northwest Iowa: An Analysis from Chan-ya-ta Site (13BV1) Buena Vista County, Iowa. Doctoral dissertation, **University Microfilms,** University of Michigan, Ann Arbor.

Vis, Robert & Dale R. Henning
1969   A Local Sequence for Mill Creek Sites in the Little Sioux Valley. **Plains Anthropologist,** Vol. 14 (46): 253-271.

Zimmerman, Larry
1971   Skadeland Mill Creek Culture Site, in Prehistoric Investigations, Marshall McKusick (ed.). **Office of the State Archaeologist, Report 3,** Iowa City.

Chapter 14

Nebraska Culture at Glenwood

Throughout the Central Plains by about A.D. 1000 there existed a series of settled farming communities whose residents built substantial earthlodge houses. In an area from northern Kansas extending into central Nebraska and west to Colorado, the archaeological remains of these communities are referred to as Upper Republican Culture. In eastern and north-central Kansas and perhaps extending northward the related Smokey Hill Culture is found. In eastern Nebraska and southwestern Iowa, similar sites exist. These are grouped into what is called the Nebraska Culture. All three of these cultures belong to what archaeologists have named the Central Plains Tradition. Although these contemporary cultures of the Central Plains Tradition may share a common cultural ancestry and exhibit a number of very similar characteristics, they differ enough to be separated into distinct groups.

Nebraska Culture sites in Iowa are concentrated in the Glenwood vicinity of Mills County. They are distributed along the ridges and bluffs and in the stream valleys of the Missouri River, Keg Creek, and Pony Creek. These locations would have been particularly favorable to horticultural groups tilling the fertile, alluvial bottomland along the river. They would have assured the presence not only of workable soil, but also of a readily available supply of water and wood for fuel and house construction.

Eighty house site locations are known in the Glenwood area. The excavation of these structures indicates that the most typical house built by Glenwood people had a square shape with rounded corners and a covered entryway which commonly faced south. These earthlodges were constructed within a semi-subterranean pit, and had walls of closely spaced vertical posts and four conical roof supports spaced around a central firepit. In some of the Glenwood houses, a wide bench was built around the central living area. Additional features of an earthlodge may have included racks for drying vegetables, storage platforms, and raised beds. Specific areas of the house were probably allocated to certain family members for sleeping. The charred timber posts found in Glenwood houses suggest that oak, black walnut, green ash, willow, plum, red cedar, and cottonwood were used for lodge and platform construction and for fuel.

Like their contemporary Plains neighbors, Glenwood people dug subterranean storage pits in the floor of their houses in order to store food and other items. These "cache pits" range in shape from shallow depressions to deep, straight-walled or bell-shaped pits. Cache pits were probably well concealed with dirt and sod in order to protect food supplies and valuables while Glenwood people were away from the village for extended periods.

The majority of Glenwood houses occur as individual homesteads or in small village clusters. None of these sites appear to have been fortified,

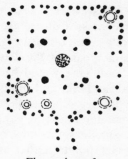

Distribution of Upper Republican and Nebraska Cultures.

Floor plan of a Nebraska Culture house.

and from this we assume that Glenwood people coexisted peacefully with their neighbors. Although few foreign items appear in Glenwood sites, the occasional occurrence of shell-tempered Oneota pottery suggests interaction with Oneota groups. Certain features of Glenwood pottery also bear similarities to ceramics of Mississippian groups in the area around the large, urban center of Cahokia in Illinois.

There is no question that Glenwood people were farmers. The location of sites near easily tillable land and the charred remains of corn, beans, sunflowers and squash in Glenwood cache pits point to horticulture as an important part of the economy. In addition, the stone and bone artifacts found are commonly those used in farming. Bone hoes were made of the scapula of both bison and elk. Some of these hoes evidently differed from the scapula hoes used by Mill Creek peoples. The placement of a notch on their lower lateral edge suggests hafting occurred further down on the blade than on those of Mill Creek. Shell hoes are also known. Knives, also made from the scapula, were probably used as in historic times to cut and process squash. Stone tools such as ground stone manos, were used to grind corn and other seeds. Stone and clay pipes suggest that tobacco was being cultivated.

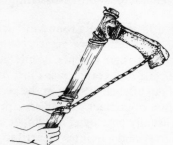

The scapula hoe used by Glenwood people.

Collared rims are one feature of some Glenwood pottery.

In addition to their farming and gathering activities, Glenwood people also hunted a number of different animals. Sites are located in areas surrounded by tall grass prairie and prairie woodlands which must have pro-

141

vided a rich habitat for a wide range of animal species. While we know that Nebraska Culture groups further to the west depended to a considerable extent on bison as a food source, bison appear to have been only a minor part of the diet for people living at Glenwood. The nearby woodlands here would have been an ideal habitat for deer, a solitary animal, and elk, and the quantity of deer and elk bone found in Glenwood houses suggests that both of these were frequently sought. The most common hunting weapon appears to have been the bow and arrow, using small, sometimes multiple-notched projectile points or larger triangular points. Other animals favored by Glenwood people include squirrel, rabbit, and smaller mammals. Wild fowl were killed, and large river fish, such as catfish and buffalo suckers, were caught using bone hooks. Single toggle-head harpoons have been found at Nebraska Culture sites and most archaeologists believe that these were probably fishing implements. The river also provided an abundant source of freshwater mussels.

A number of different tools seem to have been used in the processing of meat and dressing of hides. These include oval, triangular, and diamond-shaped stone knives, snub-nosed end scrapers and side scrapers, drills, bone awls, and hide grainers. Eyed bone needles and thread, probably of sinew, were used to sew skins together to make clothing and other items. Glenwood people had other sorts of artifacts such as antler knapping tools, hammerstones, anvils, whetstones for sharpening blades, and shaft straighteners to make their tools and keep them in working order.

Ceramics are the feature which most distinguishes Nebraska Culture sites from other Central Plains sites. Several different ceramic wares with component types have been distinguished on the basis of different rim form and decoration including: McVey, Beckman, Swoboda, and Debilka wares. It appears that in earlier Nebraska Culture sites there was a preference for collared rim forms, and later uncollared vessels became more popular. This may suggest contact with Mississippian groups at a later time, as uncollared ceramics are a characteristic of Mississippian sites.

Ceramic artifacts other than the larger utilitarian pots found in Glenwood sites include pipes, beads, scoops, and miniature vessels, some probably the work of children in imitation of their parents. While grit temper of crushed granite or a mixture of sand and granite was most frequently added to the clay, a high percentage of shell temper in the ceramics at some sites may be another indication of contact with Mississippian groups where ground clam shell was usually employed as temper.

Certain designs found on Glenwood pottery and a number of artifacts, suggest Nebraska Culture people acquired goods and ideas from other societies probably through trade. The location of their communities on Missouri River tributaries no doubt provided an access to a trade route which seems to have been as important to prehistoric communities as it was later to Euro-Americans. Periodic trading fairs may have been held at certain times of the year so that exotic items like bison robes and prized bird feathers acquired by Plains people, might be exchanged for Gulf Coast shell, Minnesota pipestone, or the pottery of eastern groups, all of which appear in Nebraska culture sites.

Throughout their existence in Iowa, Glenwood sites present a picture of peaceful, well-adapted, horticultural communities. Dates from a majority of sites, including Little Pony, Steinheimer, and Stonebrook, indicate that Glenwood people resided in southwestern Iowa for at least three centuries between A.D. 1000 and 1300. After this time we find no further trace of them in the state. A changing climate, repeated crop failure, or pressure from other groups may have brought about their emigration from Iowa. After this time it seems likely they moved westward and northward, possibly incorporating some of the traditions of the people with whom they came in contact. It is likely that the descendants of the people at Glenwood come into history as Caddoan-speaking groups such as the Arikara and Pawnee, who were first encountered by Spanish and French explorers in Nebraska and South and North Dakota.

REFERENCES

Alex, Lynn Marie
1976   Nebraska Culture at Glenwood. **Office of the State Archaeologist Educational Series 5.** Iowa City.

Anderson, Adrian
1954   Stone Artifacts from the Glenwood Area. **Journal of the Iowa Archeological Society,** Vol. 4 (2): 2-16.

Anderson, Adrian
1961   The Glenwood Sequence. **Journal of the Iowa Archeological Society,** Vol. 10 (3): 1-101.

Anderson, Duane
1975   **Western Iowa Prehistory.** Ames: Iowa State University Press.

Blakeslee, Donald (ed.)
1978   The Central Plains. **Report 11, Office of the State Archaeologist.** Iowa City.

Brown, Lionel
1967   Pony Creek Archaeology. **Publications in Salvage Archaeology 5 Smithsonian Institutions River Basin Surveys.**

Gradwohl, David
1969   Prehistoric Villages in Eastern Nebraska. **Nebraska State Historical Society Publications,** #4. Lincoln.

Gunnerson, James H.
1952   Some Nebraska Culture Pottery Types: **Plains Archaeological Conference Newsletter,** Vol. 5 (3): 39-49.

Hotopp, John
1978 "Glenwood, A Contemporary View," in The Central Plains, Donald Blakeslee (ed.), **Report 11, Office of the State Archaeologist.** Iowa City.

Ives, John
1955 Glenwood Ceramics. **Journal of the Iowa Archeological Society,** Vol. 4 (3 & 4).

McKusick, Marshall
1964 **Men of Ancient Iowa.** Ames: Iowa State University Press.

Wedel, Waldo
1961 **Prehistoric Man on the Great Plains.** Norman: University of Oklahoma Press.

Wood, Raymond (ed.)
1969 Two House Sites on the Central Plains: An Experiment in Archaeology. **Plains Anthropologist Memoir #6.**

Zimmerman, Larry
1977 Prehistoric Locational Behavior: A Computer Simulation, **Office of the State Archaeologist Report #10.** Iowa City.

Chapter 15

Oneota

Between A.D. 1000 and about A.D. 1800 most parts of Iowa were inhabited by people of the "Oneota" Culture. Oneota sites have been identified not only in Iowa but also in a broad area throughout the Midwest including the states of Illinois, Wisconsin, Minnesota, Missouri, Kansas, Nebraska, and South Dakota.

One of the most puzzling questions in midwestern archaeology is the origin of Oneota. We know that by about A.D. 1000 many midwestern groups were being influenced by the political and religious center of Cahokia. The site of Cahokia represents an urban complex covering an area about 6.5 square miles (Fowler, 1974: 6). For reasons yet to be explained, Cahokia began to decline as an important center beginning about A.D. 1150. Some archaeologists believe that it was in the migration of people outward from Cahokia that we can find the origin of Oneota. Others suggest that Oneota and Cahokia were distinct entities by A.D. 1000, but that they derived from a common Woodland cultural ancestor yet to be defined. Still others believe that Oneota culture essentially evolved from an indigenous Woodland Culture in the Upper Mississippi Valley. There is as yet no solution to this problem, and until additional evidence is forthcoming, it is likely to remain unresolved.

Distribution of Oneota sites in Iowa and surrounding states.

Most Oneota sites in Iowa are large villages, sometimes covering 100 acres or more, and typically located along large rivers and their tributaries. Cemeteries and occasionally burial mounds occur within the vicinity of the village. Along the Upper Iowa River in the northeastern part of the state we find Oneota sites such as the Elephant Terrace Cemetery, the O'Reagan Cemetery, the Flynn Cemetery, and the Lane Site. Northwestern Iowa Oneota sites include Burr Oak, Bastian, Correctionville, Dixon, Gillett Grove, and Blood Run, found along the Missouri, Big and Little Sioux rivers, and Mill Creek. The Mississippi River and its tributaries, the Flint and the Iowa in southeastern Iowa, have produced the remains of Oneota sites such as Kingston, McKinney, and Poison

145

Ivy. Finally, south central Iowa sites have been reported in the vicinity of the Red Rock Reservoir on the Des Moines River. While contact is known to have occurred between Oneota and the Nebraska Culture of the Glenwood area of southwestern Iowa, there are no well-defined Oneota sites in this region.

Unfortunately, we have very little idea of the type of house that Oneota people occupied since few actual structures have been excavated in Iowa. Sites elsewhere suggest that the house form was a long rectangle or rectangle with rounded corners. The most characteristic features found at Oneota sites are occasional hearths and bowl or bell-shaped trash and cache pits. Cache pits were dug into the house floors to allow for the storage of food, particularly corn, and other items.

Oneota people buried their dead in an extended position and placed with them a variety of artifacts. For instance, at the Flynn Cemetery in northern Allamakee County, 17 skeletons were found accompanied by artifacts such as bone whistles, pottery, chert flakes, numerous copper and brass bracelets, and beads. In one grave, the skull of a raven had been placed with the deceased. In the eye socket of the raven's skull was found a bone disc bead. We do not know the function or meaning of the raven to Oneota people but to many Native American groups this bird had special significance, and perhaps this is the case with the Oneota as well.

The most distinctive artifacts of Oneota Culture are ceramics. These have proven notoriously varied and difficult to classify, although in general they are immediately recognizable primarily for their shell temper and trailed decoration. The two major types defined to date are Correctionville Trailed and Allamakee Trailed, both shell-tempered, with Correctionville Grit Tempered a less common form.

Other Oneota artifacts tend to be less distinctive than the pottery and include items common to contemporary Plains and Prairie cultures. Chipped stone types include many tiny triangular-shaped projectile points which suggest the use of the bow and arrow as the principal weapon. Arrowheads were also fashioned from pieces of antler. A variety of stone tools such as scrapers, knives, drills, and abraders suggest the preparation of meat and the working of hides. Ground stone manos and metates were used to grind and crush seeds and nuts as well as to powder various minerals used in paint pigments. The bone of deer and bison was frequently worked into a variety of objects. Bone awls and hoes were common items.

A catlinite pipe.

One of the outstanding features of Oneota Culture was the use of red pipestone, called catlinite, which was obtained from a source in southwestern Minnesota. Catlinite was worked by Oneota people into pipes and plaques. As far as we can tell, pipes were used for smoking during ceremonial occasions. Catlinite plaques found at the Blood Run Site in Cherokee County, had been illustrated with drawings of cloven hoofed animals and designs similar to those at sites in the eastern United States.

During their early history, Oneota people seem to have spent an equal portion of their time engaged in horticulture and hunting. Corn, squash, and possibly beans and tobacco were important crops sown in gardens on the soft river floodplain where the ground was easiest to till. Wild animals such as bison and deer seem to have been important hunted forms. Fishing and the collection of wild nuts and seeds would have supplemented this diet. To carry on this lifestyle, people would probably have lived a semisedentary existence, residing in permanent villages during certain times of the year, but moving away for the summer and winter bison hunt.

With the significant change in the weather pattern throughout the Midwest which occurred at about A.D. 1200-1250, an increase in zonal westerlies resulted in drier summer conditions which probably curtailed the growing season. It would seem that this change was particularly unfavorable to horticultural groups and many people in Iowa were unable to continue their former lifestyle. Oneota people on the other hand, may have survived by becoming more dependent on hunting and less so on farming. Later Oneota sites are found further upstream and are located at higher elevations above the river. The numerous hunting tools found at these later sites and the abundance of bison bone suggests that hunting became more important once climatic conditions deteriorated.

Early Oneota sites such as Dixon, Correctionville, and Gothier have been grouped with sites of the Blue Earth River region in south central Minnesota into what is called the Correctionville-Blue Earth Phase. Judging by the date of the Dixon Site, this early phase may have begun by the tenth century A.D. Related sites are distributed over a broad area which includes locations in southeastern Nebraska, eastern Wisconsin, the Chariton River region of Kansas, and southeastern Iowa.

Later sites are represented by localities on the Iowa River and its tributaries in northeastern Iowa. These include sites like the Lane Site, Malone II Site, and the Elephant Terrace Cemetery. These appear to be related to northwest Iowa sites such as Harriman and Gillett Grove, to the southeastern McKinney Village near Toolesboro, and to sites in adjacent states. All of these have been included in what is referred to as the Orr Phase. Orr Phase materials also appear to be present at the Blood Run Site in Lyon County and the Milford Site in Dickinson County.

The Bastian Site in Cherokee County, would seem to be intermediate in time between Correctionville-Blue Earth Phase sites and Orr Phase sites, and thus serves to help link these early and late Oneota phases. Orr Phase sites date well within the late prehistoric and early historic period,

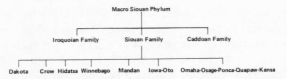

Macro Siouan Phylum

Iroquoian Family   Siouan Family   Caddoan Family

Dakota   Crow   Hidatsa   Winnebago   Mandan   Iowa-Oto   Omaha-Osage-Ponca-Quapaw-Kansa

Late Oneota sites are thought to represent the remains of historic Siouan speakers such as the Iowa and Oto. There are many divisions of the Siouan language family, and not everyone who speaks a Siouan tongue can necessarily understand another Siouan speaker. In the same way, neither can speakers of Norwegian, Persian, or English necessarily understand one another although each of these languages belongs to one Indo-European language family.

and many are believed to be the remains of villages and cemeteries of historic Siouan speaking groups in Iowa such as the Ioway and Oto.

Late Oneota sites may also represent settlements of other Siouan speakers such as the Omaha. The presence of European trade goods, such as glass beads, copper and brass jewelry, and metal cooking utensils in late Oneota sites, point to European influences reaching Siouan speakers in Iowa perhaps as early as the late 16th century.

REFERENCES

Alex, Lynn Marie
1976   Oneota. **Office of the State Archaeologist Educational Series #6.** Iowa City.

Alex, Lynn Marie
1978   The Poison Ivy Site: A New Oneota Site in Southeast Iowa. **Journal of the Iowa Archeological Society,** Vol. 25: 78-91.

Anderson, Duane
1973   Ioway Ethnohistory: A Review. Parts 1 and 2. **Annals of Iowa,** Vol. 41 (8): 1228-1241, and Vol. 42 (1): 41-59.

Anderson, Duane
1975   **Western Iowa Prehistory.** Ames: Iowa State University Press.

Bray, Robert
1961   The Flynn Cemetery: An Orr Focus Oneota Burial Site in Allamakee County. **Journal of the Iowa Archeological Society,** Vol. 10 (4): 15-25.

Fowler, Melvin
1974   Cahokia: Ancient Capital of the Midwest. **Addison-Wesley Module in Anthropology No. 48.**

Glenn, Elizabeth
1975   Physical Affiliation of the Oneota Peoples. **Office of the State Archaeologist, Report #7.** Iowa City.

Gradwohl, David
1967   A Preliminary Precis of the Moingona Phase, An Oneota Manifestation in Central Iowa. **Plains Anthropologist,** Vol. 12 (36): 211-212.

Harvey, Amy
1979   Oneota Culture in Northwestern Iowa. **Office of the State Archaeologist, Report #12.** Iowa City.

Henning, Dale
1961   Oneota Ceramics in Iowa. **Journal of the Iowa Archeological Society,** Vol. 11 (2): 1-60.

Henning, Dale
1967   Mississippian Influences on the Eastern Plains Border: An Evaluation, **Plains Anthropologist,** Vol. 12 (36): 184-194.

Henning, Dale
1970   Development and Interrelationship of Oneota Culture in the Lower Missouri River Valley. **Missouri Archaeologist,** Vol. 32: 1-180.

McKusick, Marshall
1964   **Men of Ancient Iowa.** Ames: Iowa State University Press.

McKusick, Marshall
1971   Oneota Longhouses, in Prehistoric Investigations, McKusick, Marshall(ed.). **Office of the State Archaeologist,** Report #3. Iowa City.

McKusick, Marshall
1973   The Grant Oneota Village. **Office of the State Archaeologist, Report #4.** Iowa City.

Mott, Mildred
1938   The Relation of Historic Indian Tribes to Archaeological Manifestations in Iowa. **Iowa Journal of History and Politics,** Vol. 36 (3): 227-304.

Skinner, Alanson
1915   Societies of the Iowa, Kansa, and Ponca Indians. **Anthropological Papers of the American Museum of Natural History,** Vol. 11, Part 9: 679-740.

Skinner, Alanson
1926   Ethnology of the Iowa Indians. **Milwaukee Museum Bulletin,** Vol. 5 (4): 181-354.

Slattery, Richard and George Horton
1975   The McKinney Village Site: An Oneota Site in Southeastern Iowa. **Journal of the Iowa Archeological Society,** Vol. 22: 35-61.

Slattery, Richard
1979   Further Testing at the McKinney Oneota Village Site (13LA1). **Journal of the Iowa Archeological Society,** Vol. 26: 81-94.

Straffin, Dean
1971   The Kingston Oneota Site. **Office of the State Archaeologist Report #2,** Iowa City.

Tiffany, Joseph
1978   An Overview of Oneota Sites in Southeast Iowa: A Perspective from the Ceramic Analysis of the Schmeizer Site, 13DM10, Des Moines County, Iowa. Paper given at the 1978 annual meeting of the Iowa Academy of Sciences.

Wedel, Mildred Mott
1959   Oneota Sites on the Upper Iowa River. **Missouri Archaeologist,** Vol. 21 (2-4).

Wedel, Mildred Mott
1961   Indian Villages on the Upper Iowa River. **Palimpsest,** Vol. 42 (21): 56-592.

Wedel, Mildred Mott
1961   Ethnohistory: Its Payoffs and Pitfalls for Iowa Archaeologists. **Journal of the Iowa Archeological Society,** Vol. 23: 1-44.

Wedel, Mildred Mott
1978   A Synonymy of Names for the Iowa Indians. **Journal of the Iowa Archeological Society,** Vol. 25: 49-77.

Chapter 16

Preservation and Conservation

We have come a long way in archaeology since the days when the moundbuilder problem was the focus of antiquarian concern. Iowa's prehistoric outline has been established and each new site provides information to help in our reconstruction of the past. Nevertheless, our increasing knowledge has, in some cases, been surpassed by the rate of destruction of archaeological sites.

Over the past century, the expansion of our population with the concomitant growth of towns and cities, agricultural development, and elaboration of communication networks has caused a loss of prehistoric and historic resources. Often modern buildings and highways are constructed in locations which were equally appealing to prehistoric people, resulting in the disruption of areas having a high density of sites. Farming has had a bittersweet effect on archaeological remains. The plow has brought to the surface evidence of sites which might not have been discovered. Thanks to many farmers the importance of these remains was recognized and brought to the attention of archaeologists. At the same time, the context of artifacts has been disturbed, and some sites, particularly mounds, have been obliterated as a result of farming activities.

The future may bring a new threat. Our increasing demand for greater supplies of domestic fuel poses the danger of large scale land disturbance. Coal strip mines, like those being developed in southern Iowa, or uranium and taconite exploration now underway in our western states, may create the greatest threat to archaeological sites yet. While many mining companies are sensitive to the importance of prehistoric remains, the necessity of producing expedient, domestic sources of energy may outweigh their good intentions.

At the same time, sites are lost to age-old forces of destruction. Erosion from wind and water takes its toll on archaeological remains. The damming of rivers with the raising and lowering of the water for flood control and irrigation has accelerated natural stream erosion in many cases. The destruction of sites as a result of human looting continues to plague us. A market for prehistoric artifacts has provided the impetus for much of this looting. No matter how innocent their motives, whenever someone purchases archaeological remains they contribute to the wanton destruction of sites. If no one bought artifacts, a market would not exist, and the rate of site destruction would decline.

Up until the 1960's our prehistoric and historic sites were protected only minimally by law. Were it not for the support of a few conscientious individuals and private organizations, particularly the Iowa Archeological Society, many important sites would have been lost. Since its establishment in 1951, the I.A.S. and its individual chapters have located and helped to salvage a number of sites. Thanks to the Society and the project director, Adrian Anderson, the Kulbolm Site, a Nebraska Culture site at Glenwood, was excavated before it was incorporated into a feed lot. Likewise, an irrigation system was delayed at the Skadeland Mill Creek Site until the information the site contained was recovered by Society members working with Larry Zimmerman, then a student at The University of Iowa, and funded by small grants from the University and the Sanford Museum. Unfortunately, during this same period, many recorded sites were lost due to a lack of financial support needed to salvage or protect them.

In the late 1960's, prehistoric and historic remains came to be recognized as valuable **cultural resources,** as important in their own right as other of our natural resources including wildlife, parks, wilderness areas, and mineral supplies. Since that time, various pieces of federal legislation designed to promote the recording and protection of cultural resources on federal lands, or on land where a federal project or federally financed project is planned, have created new safeguards for the protection of prehistoric and historic sites. They have also resulted in increased funding for research, protection, and restoration of such sites. (See Appendix 2) In the last ten years, a whole new field of cultural resources management has evolved which functions to compromise the interests of development and industry with those of conservation and protection.

The State Historic Preservation Office and the Office of the State Archaeologist are responsible for instigating cultural resources surveys when federal projects which will disturb the ground, such as flood control, dam building, highway construction, mining, and so on, are planned. This research, part of broader Environmental Impact Studies, is designed to evaluate the impact of a proposed project on natural and cultural resources. Archaeologists are hired to undertake a survey of the project area in order to locate and record any cultural resources present. The significance of the recorded sites is determined and recommendations offered. Where important sites are found, salvage excavation may be recommended. In this way, remains which might have been destroyed by the project itself are recovered, and their context and association recorded. The site is now gone, but the information it contained has been saved.

Some sites, judged too important to be lost to excavation or to the project, are recommended for protection. Sometimes the project can be altered in order to preserve these sites. Such was the case in Iowa with the Little Maquoketa Mounds, the Keller Mounds, and the Siouxland Sand and Gravel Site.

Historic and prehistoric sites deemed worthy of national recognition can be nominated to the National Register of Historic Places. This insures protection of important sites and makes them eligible for federal funding to be used in restoration and maintenance. The prehistoric Hopewellian mounds at Toolesboro are on the National Register, and our historic Old Capitol in Iowa City has been elected a National Historic Landmark. The latter is a good example of an historic site which is still in use. This is not only conservation-minded, it is economical as well. Certainly a building of this quality could not be constructed for the price of its restoration.

The federal preservation legislation of the 1960's and 1970's has been overwhelmingly beneficial in the location and protection of cultural resources in Iowa. Some federal agencies, or agencies receiving federal funding working in the state, have their own employees and programs that deal specifically with cultural resources and the impact of their projects on them. As a result of these efforts, and federal sponsorship, sites such as the Cherokee Sewer Site, the F.T.D. Site, the Saylorville Reservoir sites, and many Nebraska Culture earthlodges have been salvaged or protected.

The preservation of cultural resources on state and private lands has been more difficult to insure. In Iowa, antiquities on state-owned land are not specifically protected by state law. State law provides for the existence of the Office of the State Archaeologist, whose function it is to oversee the documentation and protection of Iowa antiquities, and to maintain a repository for prehistoric materials and records pertaining to Iowa sites. The Office is also charged with informing and involving the public in the preservation of cultural resources.

The State Preserves Advisory Board, established in 1965, provides a mechanism for dedicating areas with significant floral and faunal, geological, archaeological, scenic, or historic resources into the state system. As a result of this program, prehistoric sites such as the Turkey River Mounds, and historic remains like Ft. Atkinson have been designated preserves and are afforded the highest level of protection available. Other sites like the Effigy Mounds have been incorporated into national or state parks, making it unlawful to vandalize or destroy them.

The growing consciousness and activism among Native Americans has also contributed to the conservation of the Indian heritage. Euro-Americans in particular mourn the loss of written history since it is the key to their own heritage and to the origin of modern American society. The destruction of an original document such as the Declaration of Independence would be sadly felt by most. This has not been the case when a prehistoric mound or village site is destroyed. The Native American past is retrievable only through oral tradition and in the material remains left at prehistoric and early historic sites. Unless these sites can be located and preserved, the information they contain is lost.

During the 1960's and 1970's, several incidents in Iowa and elsewhere throughout the country illustrated the differential treatment extended to historic versus prehistoric sites. For many years now, Euro-Americans have consciously fought to restore and protect colonial and 19th century structures. It was also unlawful to disturb or vandalize historic cemeteries. Prehistoric sites, on the other hand, including those containing human remains, were not afforded such protection. The entire period when the moundbuilder problem dominated prehistoric resea~~ plifies the disregard for the cultural heritage of Native A However, in 1978, a bill was passed in Iowa's legislature m third degree misdemeanor for an individual to intentionally human remains from any burial site without lawful authority.

also provides for the reburial of those human remains unavoidably disturbed. Our U.S. Constitution declares equality under the law to all citizens. The new Antiquities legislation now extends the same respect and protection afforded Euro-American cemeteries to those of prehistoric Native Americans. Furthermore, the State Archaeologist has the power to deny permission to disinter ancient human remains demonstrated to be significant from the standpoint of scientific or historical importance.

Sites on private lands have almost no legal protection in Iowa. Only where the landowner is conscious of the importance of such remains and conscientious about their care, is protection available. In Iowa, we are fortunate in having a public which, in general, is sensitive to the historic and prehistoric past. Many sites have been salvaged and are being maintained by these private "stewards" of the land.

Nevertheless, while some people are aware of the importance of prehistoric remains others are not. Antiques and old buildings are more familiar objects to modern Americans and readily gain their appreciation. Potsherds and stone tools are uncommon and may seem strange and insignificant. Only by becoming familiar with these important resources and informing others about them, can we hope to insure their protection. All of us can learn to recognize and record archaeological sites. By helping others recognize and understand them we may learn when they are endangered and can take measures to salvage and protect them. This is our best safeguard for the conservation of cultural resources, especially those on private lands.

Archaeological sites on state and federal properties can continue to gain protection through legislation at the local and national level. If we are aware that these sites exist before they are threatened, we can support legislation which will preserve and protect them. In emergency situations, a call to the State Archaeologist, the State Historic Preservation Officer, or a telegram to a local representative or congressman, usually brings immediate results.

REFERENCES

Anderson, Duane
1975 **Western Iowa Prehistory.** Ames: Iowa State University Press.

Anderson, Duane **et. al.**
1978 The Lewis Central School (13PW5): A Resolution of Ideological Conflicts at an Archaic Ossuary in Western Iowa. **Plains Anthropologist,** Vol. 23 (81): 183-219.

Anderson, Duane **et. al.**
1979 The Siouxland Sand and Gravel Site (13WD402): New Data and the Application of Iowa's New State Law Protecting Ancient Cemeteries. **Journal of the Iowa Archeological Society,** Vol. 26: 121-145.

Illinois Dept. of Transportation
1978   Preservation Archaeology, Interstate 270.

Lipe, William
1974   A Conservation Model for American Archaeology. **The Kiva.**
       Vol. 39 (3 & 4): 213-245.

McGimsey, Charles R.
1972   **Public Archaeology.** New York: Seminar Press Inc.

McGimsey, Charles R.
n.d.   Archaeology and Archaeological Resources: A Guide for those
       Planning to Use, Affect, or Alter the Lands Surface. **Society for
       American Archaeology.** Washington, D.C.

McGimsey, Charles, Hester Davis and Carl Chapman
n.d.   Stewards of the Past. Extension Division. Columbia: University
       of Missouri.

McMillan, R. Bruce
1972   Archaeology During the Eleventh Hour. **Midwest Museum Con-
       ference Quarterly,** Vol. 32.

Riggle, Stanley
1979   The Role of Environmental Review in Iowa Archaeology. **Journal
       of the Iowa Archeological Society,** Vol. 26: 97-118.

Tiffany, Joseph
1978   Archaeological Preserves in Iowa: A Report Prepared for the
       State Preserves Advisory Board. **Research Papers 3:1,** Office of
       the State Archaeologist. Iowa City.

Chapter 17

Opportunities in Archaeology

As we have seen, archaeologists are people who reconstruct the past through the systematic recovery and interpretation of the material remains left by former societies. In this concluding chapter we will learn some of the steps one can take to become an archaeologist, whether the intention is to make it into a career or an interesting hobby.

Archaeology as a Career

A professional career in archaeology is the culmination of several years of university education, specialized training, and field and laboratory experience. In the United States, people who intend to become professional archaeologists usually receive their Bachelor's, Master's, and Doctoral degrees in anthropology with an emphasis on archaeology. This is because archaeology is considered a part of anthropology. It shares with all of anthropology the emphasis on the importance of culture, and a holistic approach (historical, comparative, and integrated) to the study of *Homo sapiens* as a biological and cultural species. During their university years, students of archaeology will take classes in other subjects related to their field of study. Background and training in geology, zoology, chemistry, soil science, history, languages, statistics, museology and many others may have direct bearing on their ability to observe and describe what they discover in the field and laboratory, and to interpret their findings. As we have seen, archaeological research has become increasingly interdisciplinary in nature, and it is imperative that the person in charge of a project know how much of his research will require the assistance of specialists in other fields.

While in college, a student should have many opportunities to participate on survey and excavation projects. This experience will help prepare him for future research on his own. No one can become competent in archaeology without doing it. A student's field work is not only an academic and practical exercise, it is a lesson in human relations. A good project director will have to know how to prepare a field setting in which a small group of sometimes very diverse individuals may have to work and live in close quarters, sometimes without outside contact, for considerable periods of time.

By the time most people reach graduate school they have decided on a particular area of archaeology in which to specialize. They usually have chosen the prehistory of a certain geographical and cultural area, and may decide to become especially proficient in one or two areas of study such as faunal, ceramic, or lithic analysis. In addition to these individual specialities, in order to receive a doctoral degree, students are expected to be familiar with all areas of archaeological analysis, and to have the background necessary to design and implement complex research projects and to analyze, interpret, and synthesize their results.

In Iowa, at least four of our academic institutions offer a Bachelor's degree in anthropology: The University of Iowa in Iowa City, Iowa State University at Ames, the University of Northern Iowa in Cedar Falls, and Luther College in Decorah. The University of Iowa and Iowa State University also provide a Master's Degree program in anthropology with an emphasis on archaeology. The only institution in the state offering the PhD. is The University of Iowa. The chairman of the anthropology department in each of these schools can furnish detailed information on their respective programs.

While some employment opportunities exist for the student with a Bachelor's or Master's degree in anthropology, these are limited, often to field positions. The person contemplating a career in archaeology should aim at least for the Master's degree.

In the past ten years, federal legislation requiring cultural resources surveys has expanded employment possibilities for people with a Bachelor's or Master's degree, however, the PhD. is required for almost all other areas of occupation, particularly University teaching and research. A few jobs exist for archaeologists in museums, the National Park Service, secondary schools, or rarely with a well known organization such as the Smithsonian Institution, but these are scarce, and competition is strong. In addition, some of these areas require additional training in specific areas such as museology, resource management, education, and so on.

The Office of the State Archaeologist in conjunction with The University of Iowa offers three correspondence courses relating to Iowa prehistory. These are: "An Introduction to Midwestern Prehistory: Emphasis Iowa" (113:20), "Iowa Prehistory" (113:182), and "History of Iowa Archaeology" (113:80). The first is designed as an introductory course for people with a general interest in Iowa prehistory. The latter two are intended for people with some university experience. For anyone interested in Iowa prehistory, or for those contemplating a career in archaeology, these courses are recommended. Further information is available from:

Guided Correspondence Study
W 400 East Hall
The University of Iowa
Iowa City, Iowa 52242.

Archaeology for Everyone

Even if a professional career is not planned, there are many ways the lay archaeologist can keep in touch and become involved in the field. The Iowa Archeological Society offers the best opportunities. The Society is an organization of people interested in learning about and protecting prehistoric remains. It publishes a quarterly newsletter describing local

157

finds throughout the state, book reviews, and archaeological happenings. An annual journal contains more extensive articles on various aspects of Iowa prehistory. The Society holds an annual meeting where lay and professional archaeologists gather to share information, display their finds, and discuss Iowa prehistory. Individual chapters sponsor regular meetings where they hear speakers, view interesting slide presentations and films, and plan field projects. Information on membership in the Society is available through the Office of the State Archaeologist of Iowa.

Since 1976, the Society in conjunction with the Office of the State Archaeologist and The University of Iowa, has offered a field school in archaeology for Society members. Each year an excavation of a site in Iowa is conducted and members have the opportunity to participate over a series of long weekends. This is the most direct way an individual can gain excavation experience and training in a supervised, field situation. The hours spent in the field can be credited to the individual's certification. A certain amount of laboratory experience is also provided during the project.

The Iowa Archaeological Certification Program has been in existence since 1977. The program is conducted by the Office of the State Archaeologist in cooperation with the Iowa Archeological Society. The objectives of the program are:

1. to train a group of individuals to assist professional archaeologists in field and laboratory work.
2. to increase the frequency of site reporting in the state and to upgrade the quality of site reports.
3. to stress the importance of the well planned, orderly, and controlled survey and excavation, and thus discourage pothunting, and unprofessional weekend "digs."
4. to involve capable and interested individuals in the location and preservation of Iowa's prehistoric resources.

Any Society member may enter the certification program. A person may become certified as a site surveyor, field technician, or laboratory technician. Some people have become certified in all three. Certification is awarded after the individual has shown proficiency in one of the three categories.

Certification qualifies an individual to assist in the location of prehistoric remains and the analysis of recovered materials. A certified surveyor, for example, could help check out cultural resources in areas threatened by construction. A field technician would be qualified to act as a crew member on supervised excavations. The certified laboratory technician could be called upon to analyze archaeological materials. The certification program is also an excellent way for individuals to learn how to record sites in their local area and how to organize home collections.

In addition to the certification program and field school, the Office of the State Archaeologist has an organized program in public education. This program has developed a series of educational pamphlets on Iowa prehistory, a number of films on various aspects of prehistory and history in our state, and a series referred to as the P.A.S.T. program (Programming Archaeology for School Teachers). The P.A.S.T. program is a series of ten filmstrips with accompanying scripts on cassette tapes about Iowa prehistory. The series includes a set of scripts appropriate to younger audiences and accompanied by a teacher's manual, as well as a set for high school age and adult audiences. This *Handbook* was written as part of the P.A.S.T. project, and is designed to supplement the adult filmstrip and cassette series. Information on all of these materials can be acquired by contacting the: Office of the State Archaeologist, Eastlawn, University of Iowa, Iowa City, Iowa 52422.

In addition to the above sources, information on Iowa prehistory and history can be gained by contacting the State Historic Preservation Office, Division of Historic Preservation, 26 East Market Street, Iowa City, Iowa 52240; Historical Society of Iowa, 402 Iowa Ave., Iowa City, 52240; or local museums and county historical societies.

Field opportunities in other states and abroad, are published annually by the Archaeological Institute of America in their "Fieldwork Opportunities Bulletin," a copy of which is available through the Archaeological Institute of America, 53 Park Place, New York, New York 10007.

If you are interested in archaeology and Iowa prehistory, do something about it. Read a book, borrow a film or filmstrip from the Office of the State Archaeologist, join the Iowa Archeological Society, or write one of our Iowa colleges about their programs. To many, archaeology remains an exotic, fascinating, and essentially alien field. Yet, this need not be the case. There is a role for everyone. Familiarity with its hard work, tedious details, and sometimes less than spectacular results, seldom breeds disappointment. For just about everyone actively involved, archaeology is rarely dull, sometimes exciting, and always unpredictable.

REFERENCES

Rowe, John W.
1958 Archaeology as a Career. **Journal of the Iowa Archeological Society,** Vol. 7: 17-33.

Glossary

ACTIVITY AREA: a concentration of artifacts and/or features whose provenience suggests the occurrence of a particular activity at that part of the site.

AERIAL PHOTOGRAPH: a photograph taken from above, usually from an airplane or balloon, showing the land surface. It is useful in demonstrating the existence of those archaeological sites recognizable through unusual surface features such as mounds, depressions, or zones of differentially colored vegetation.

ANTHROPOLOGY: the study of the human species.

ARCHAEOLOGY: the scientific study of extinct cultures through the systematic recovery and interpretation of the material remains left by past societies.

ARTIFACTS: objects humanly altered or manufactured.

ASSEMBLAGE: all of the various classes of artifacts found together at a site.

BENCH MARK (DATUM POINT): the permanent reference point(s) established at a site used in determining the vertical and horizontal relationship of all finds.

CERAMICS: pottery artifacts.

COUNTY PLAT BOOK: a publication which shows the location of property in a township and its owners.

CULTURE: all of the patterns for living which humans have created in adapting to their environment and which are transmitted from one generation to another through means of behavior, symbols, and artifacts.

DIRECT HISTORICAL APPROACH: a method of working back from the historic into the prehistoric period by identifying the archaeological sites of known historic groups and using diagnostic artifacts from these sites to determine the ethnic identity of other sites where similar remains are found.

ETHNOLOGY: the study of existing cultures, or those recently extinct.

EXCAVATION: uncovering or exposing a prehistoric or historic site by digging.

FAUNA: refers to animals. Faunal remains from archaeological sites usually consist of bone, teeth, shell, and scales.

FLORA: refers to plants. Floral remains from archaeological sites usually consist of pollen, charred seeds, charred wood, and phytoliths.

GRID: a series of intersecting lines which form a series of squares across a site and which facilitates the mapping of all finds so as to demonstrate their vertical and horizontal relationships.

HISTORICAL ARCHAEOLOGY: the scientific study of cultures from the historic period (after written records) through the systematic recovery and interpretation of their material remains.

HUMAN PALEONTOLOGY: the study of prehistoric human skeletal remains.

IN SITU: in place, undisturbed.

INTRUSION: where the remains from one culture or period of occupation at a site have become displaced and occur out of context and mixed with those of another at the same site.

INTERDISCIPLINARY APPROACH: an integrated effort by scientists from several disciplines working together to recover, analyze, and interpret archaeological remains.

LAW OF SUPERPOSITION: the rule which assumes that the lowest levels (strata) at a site are older than those which lie on top.

LEVELING ROD OR STADIA ROD: a graduated rod marked off in feet or meters, used with a transit or alidade in measuring the depth and distance of finds in a site.

LINE LEVEL: an instrument for determining whether a line stretched between two points is on a horizontal plane. It consists of a glass tube partially filled with alcohol so as to leave an air bubble that moves to the exact center of the tube when the instrument is on a horizontal plane.

LITHICS: stone artifacts.

MALACOLOGIST: a scientist who studies molluscs or snails.

MULTI-COMPONENT: several periods of occupation or cultures represented at one site.

PALEOBOTANIST: a scientist who studies prehistoric plant life.

PALEONTOLOGIST: a scientist who studies prehistoric animal life.

PALYNOLOGIST: a scientist who studies pollen.

PEDESTAL: the small earthen mounds on which a find is left while the level around it is excavated. By leaving all finds from a particular level exposed on pedestals, it is possible to photograph and map them in order to see their relationship before they are removed from the excavation.

PROTOHISTORY: the period of incipient history. In North America it refers to the time after early European contact had been made but where large sections of the country were unknown or known only through second-hand or sketchy accounts.

PREHISTORIC ARCHAEOLOGY: the study of the material remains of societies which existed prior to written documentation.

PROFILE OR SECTION: a drawing showing the vertical location of strata and finds in an excavated square.

PLUMB-BOB: a brass weight (or equivalent) suspended from a cord (plumb line) and used to determine the exact location of a find straight down from two intersecting tapes.

PROVENIENCE: the context of artifacts and features including their location and relationship to others.

RADIOCARBON DATING: a method of dating organic remains from archaeological sites 50,000 to 1,000 years old. It is based on the fact that living organisms incorporate known amounts of radioactive carbon (C14) as part of their carbon dioxide intake (in plants through photosynthesis; in animals by feeding on plants). When the organism dies, the radiocarbon disintegrates at a known rate. It is possible to calculate the age of the organic remains by measuring the amount of C14 remaining in the sample.

REVERSED STRATIGRAPHY: where the normal sequence of stratigraphy has been reversed so that the most recent levels are on the bottom and the oldest at the top.

SERIATION: the ordering of artifact types from several sites so that their frequency reflects a battle-ship shaped curve of rising popularity, peak popularity, and declining popularity.

SINGLE COMPONENT: one period of occupation at a site.

SITE: any location that shows evidence of human occupation.

SKIM-SHOVELING: the removal of thin soil layers by making shallow cuts with a shovel.

STRATIGRAPHY: the successive layers of natural and cultural levels at a site.

SURVEY: the deliberate search for prehistoric or historic sites.

TOPOGRAPHIC MAP: a map showing the natural and manmade features of the land surface.

Appendix A:

Archaeological Site Survey Procedures for Filing Site Sheets and Assigning Accession Numbers

GENERAL INFORMATION

The site record sheet you turn in to the Office of the State Archaeologist (OSA) goes through several steps before it is returned to you with a typed copy. First, it is checked against existing information to insure the site has never been reported before. If the site has been reported previously, it is assigned the same number as the original report and added to the county files as a **Supplemental Sheet.** If not, it is given a site number and recorded in the confidential inventory kept at the Office. Next, the site report is typed in triplicate and the map is xeroxed from your topographic map or is traced on the back of each copy. One copy is filed at OSA in the county book, one copy is sent to Historic Preservation as a duplicate should our files be destroyed, and the final copy is given to you along with your original. Please check the typed copy for any errors that may have been made in transcription and report any problems. There are several things you can do to help facilitate the entire process:

SITE SHEETS

1. Fill out the site record sheet **in ink as completely and as carefully as possible.** This should include Tenant and/or Owner (preferably while at the site), Present Condition, Other Material Reported, and Recommendations.

On the site sheet, item #8 is the **location** of the site and should be a detailed description of the site in relation to roads, streams, fences, houses, etc. Include the direction and distance from these landmarks to the site. On item #11, **please** list the artifacts collected. A "yes" or "no" will not suffice. Instead, state what was found and the number of each item.

For example: Stone: 30 waste flakes, 2 projectile points, 1 biface
Pottery: 2 Late Woodland bodysherds, 6 Oneota rim-sherds

The new site sheet combines the best of the previous forms and gives ample opportunity to fully describe a site. If you have more to report, please use the space for Remarks on the back. If you have questions, ask. Incomplete or illegible forms **will be returned.** Correct locational information is crucial to good site reporting. As more and more sites are being reported in Iowa, the location of a site to the fourth or fifth quarter becomes very important. Please see the attached sheet entitled "Locating Sites Within A Section," for an explanation of the four-quarter system.

2. If at all possible, please use a topographic map to plot your sites. Topographic maps are much more accurate and the sites can be drawn to their correct size and placement. When you send in your site sheets, just xerox the indicated portion of your topographic map and enclose the xeroxed copy with your site sheets. If you cannot xerox the map, please trace the roads, rivers, houses, and the elevation line(s) on which the site is located. Topographic maps can be obtained through our office.

If you use a hand-drawn map, **please** use felt-tip or ink pens to draw your maps. A light table is used for tracing, and a pencil-drawn map is nearly invisible when it comes to tracing. Make your map as complete as possible: name roads, rivers, streams, cemeteries, and buildings and indicate bluffs, ridges, terraces and fields. Indicate where the site is located to correct size and placement. Aerial photographs may be used in place of maps if they are available. State the scale of your map. If you have traced your map from a U.S.G.S. quadrangle sheet, a flood prone survey map or some other source, please indicate this information on the map side of the site sheet and the name of the map used on the front side.

3. If several sites are in one section, these may be placed on the first site sheet map of the group. The other site sheets can refer to the first map. Mark each site with a consecutive number or letter and be sure to put this same number or letter on each site sheet in the space next to Official Site Number. For example, if you have three sites in Section 3, R14W, T85N, Tama County, fill out three site reports and label them A, B, and C. Use a topographic map or draw a map of Sec. 3 and attach it to the site sheet for Site A. Plot the three sites on the map, label them A, B, and C and then indicate on the site sheets for B and C that the map can be found with site sheet A. This may be done **only** if the sites are in **one** section. Please do not put **several sections** on one hand-drawn map. Several sections **may** be included on the xeroxed copy of a topographic map.

Please send completed site reports to:

    Site Records
    Office of State Archaeologist
    Eastlawn Building
    University of Iowa
    Iowa City, Iowa 52242

4. Avoid confusing abbreviations whenever possible.

5. Ask for site numbers and accession numbers. **Do not assign yourself a number.**

ACCESSION NUMBERS

1. Accession numbers will only be given if the collection is present at the Office of the State Archaeologist. Collections in amateur hands or out of the office will be assigned a number when they are brought in. After being assigned an accession number by OSA, the collection then becomes the property of OSA. Special situations will be considered on a case by case basis.

2. If a collection is turned in when the initial site sheet is prepared, an accession number will be assigned at the same time as the site number.

3. If a collection is turned in after the original site sheet, it will be assigned an accession number at that time. It will also be necessary to fill out a site sheet to accompany the collection. This will be filed in the proper county book as a supplemental site sheet to the original one.

SITE NAMING

The procedures for naming sites have been changed. Only sites which are excavated or are known to have a locally used name will be given a site name. When turning in a site sheet, list a Local Site Name **only** if the people in the area use that name. If there is no name, such as for a newly discovered surface collection, do **not** give it a name. Therefore, most of the sites reported will not have a site name.

IOWA SITE RECORD

OFFICE SITE NUMBER _____

ACCESSION NUMBER _____

1. County _____ Local site name _____
2. Range _____ Township _____ Section _____
3. On the _____ ¼ , _____ ¼ , _____ ¼ , _____ ¼ , _____ ¼ .
   _____ ¼ , _____ ¼ , _____ ¼ , _____ ¼ , _____ ¼ .
4. Type of site _____ Maps used _____
5. Tenant _____ Address _____
6. Owner _____ Address _____
7. Informant _____ Address _____
8. General location of site in relation to streams, bluffs, river terraces, including modern
   landmarks such as roads and houses.

   _____
   _____
   _____
   _____
   _____
   _____
   _____ Estimated site size _____
9. Present condition _____
10. Previous excavations _____
    By whom _____ Address _____
11. Material collected: a. Bone _____
    b. Stone _____
    c. Pottery _____
    d. Other _____
    Owner _____ Address _____
12. Method of collection _____
13. Other material reported _____
    Owner _____ Address _____
14. Recommendations _____
15. References _____
16. Recorded by _____ Address _____

    Contract Completion Report/
17. Date recorded _____ Research Paper _____

Sketch of map of location

Range _____ Township _____ Section _____

Indicate the chief topographical features, such as streams and elevations. Also indicate houses and roads. Indicate the site location by enclosing the site area with dotted line.

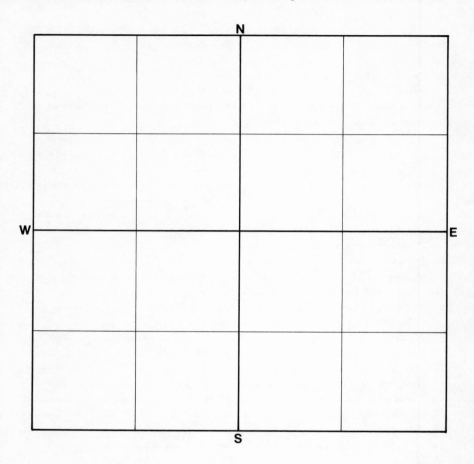

Notes:

LOCATING SITES WITHIN A SECTION

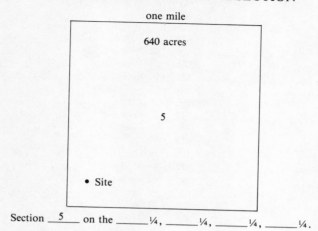

one mile

640 acres

5

• Site

Section __5__ on the _____ ¼, _____ ¼, _____ ¼, _____ ¼.

First Division

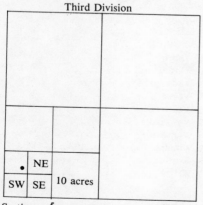

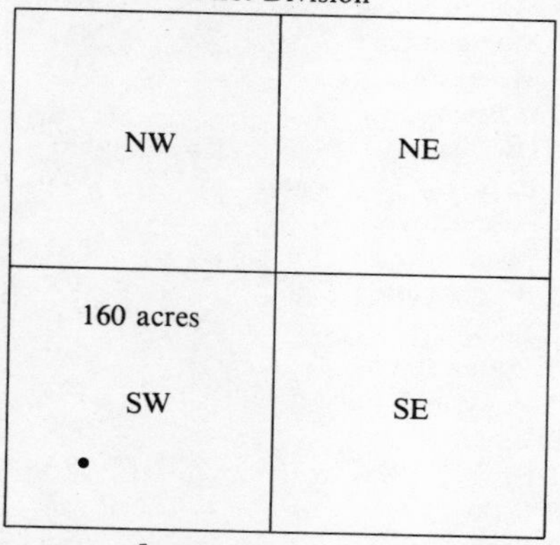

NW   NE

160 acres

SW   SE

•

Section __5__ on the _____ ¼, _____ ¼, _____ ¼ _SW_ ¼.

Second Division

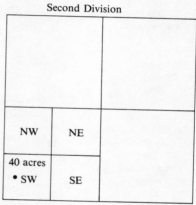

NW   NE

40 acres
• SW   SE

Section __5__ on the _____ ¼, _____ ¼, _SW_ ¼, _SW_ ¼.

Third Division

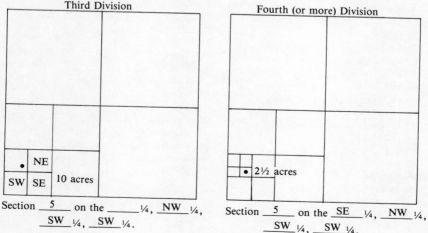

• NE
SW SE 10 acres

Section __5__ on the _____ ¼, _NW_ ¼, _SW_ ¼, _SW_ ¼.

Fourth (or more) Division

• 2½ acres

Section __5__ on the _SE_ ¼, _NW_ ¼, _SW_ ¼, _SW_ ¼.

COUNTY ABBREVIATIONS FOR
SITE DESIGNATION

1	Adair	AD	51	Jefferson	JF
2	Adams	AA	52	Johnson	JH
3	Allamakee	AM	53	Jones	JN
4	Appanoose	AN	54	Keokuk	KK
5	Audubon	AB	55	Kossuth	KH
6	Benton	BE	56	Lee	LE
7	Black Hawk	BH	57	Linn	LN
8	Boone	BN	58	Louisa	LA
9	Bremer	BM	59	Lucas	LC
10	Buchanan	BC	60	Lyon	LO
11	Buena Vista	BV	61	Madison	MD
12	Butler	BT	62	Mahaska	MK
13	Calhoun	CH	63	Marion	MA
14	Carroll	CR	64	Marshall	MR
15	Cass	CA	65	Mills	ML
16	Cedar	CD	66	Mitchell	MT
17	Cerro Gordo	CE	67	Monona	MN
18	Cherokee	CK	68	Monroe	MO
19	Chickasaw	CW	69	Montgomery	MM
20	Clarke	CL	70	Muscatine	MC
21	Clay	CY	71	O'Brien	OB
22	Clayton	CT	72	Osceola	OA
23	Clinton	CN	73	Page	PA
24	Crawford	CF	74	Palo Alto	PL
25	Dallas	DA	75	Plymouth	PM
26	Davis	DV	76	Pocahontas	PT
27	Decatur	DT	77	Polk	PK
28	Delaware	DW	78	Pottawattamie	PW
29	Des Moines	DM	79	Poweshiek	PH
30	Dickinson	DK	80	Ringgold	RN
31	Dubuque	DB	81	Sac	SA
32	Emmet	ET	82	Scott	ST
33	Fayette	FT	83	Shelby	SH
34	Floyd	FD	84	Sioux	SX
35	Franklin	FN	85	Story	SR
36	Fremont	FM	86	Tama	TM
37	Green	GR	87	Taylor	TA
38	Grundy	GN	88	Union	UN
39	Guthrie	GT	89	Van Buren	VB
40	Hamilton	HM	90	Wapello	VP
41	Hancock	HK	91	Warren	WA
42	Hardin	HA	92	Washington	WS
43	Harrison	HR	93	Wayne	WE
44	Henry	HN	94	Webster	WB
45	Howard	HW	95	Winnebago	WN
46	Humboldt	HB	96	Winneshiek	WH
47	Ida	IA	97	Woodbury	WD
48	Iowa	IW	98	Worth	WT
49	Jackson	JK	99	Wright	WR
50	Jasper	JP			

Appendix B:
Federal and State Laws Pertaining to Antiquities in Iowa

Federal
— Public Law 59-209 (Antiquities Act of 1906)
— Public Law 74-292 (Historic Sites Act of 1935)
— Public Law 89-665 and Public Law 94-458 amending the former (National Historic Preservation Act of 1966)
— Public Law 86-523 (Reservoir Salvage Act of 1960)
— Public Law 91-190 (National Environmental Policy Act of 1969)
— Public Law 93-291 (Preservation of Historic and Archaeological Data Act of 1974)
— Executive Order 11593 ("Protection and Enhancement of the Cultural Environment" 1971)
— Interim Policy for 93-291
— Title 36 Code of Federal Regulations —
  Parts — 60
         — 61
         — 63
         — 66
         — 800
             — flow chart for Part 800
             — ACHP's No Adverse Effect Guidelines
— Title 7 CFR Part 656
— additional action to 7 CFR 656
— an additional action to 7 CFR 656
— 7 CFR Part 1901
— 33 CFR 305
— Bureau of Outdoor Recreation (now HCRS) — Part 640 grant-in-aid series
— Memo 52 by Environmental Protection Agency

State (Iowa Code)
305 A State Archaeologist; Ancient Cemeteries; State Site Inventory
303 State Historical Department
111.B State Preserves Advisory Board
111.2 Iowa Conservation Commission